MAMMALS
of the
ADIRONDACKS

William K. Chapman
with Dennis Aprill

Published
North Country B
Utica, New

D1529251

ISBN 0-932052-61-4

Printed and bound in Hong Kong

Library of Congress Cataloging-in-Publication Data

Chapman, William K., 1951-
    Mammals of the Adirondacks/by William K. Chapman with Dennis
Aprill.
        p.   c.m.
    Includes indexes.
    ISBN 0-932052-61-4
    1. Mammals—New York (State)—Adirondack Park—Identification.
    2. Mammals—New York (State)—Adirondack Mountains Region—
Identification. I. Aprill, Dennis. II. Title.
    QL719.N7C48   1991
    599.09747'5—dc20   90-28881
                                                        CIP

Book design by John Mahaffy

North Country Books, Inc.
Utica, New York

TABLE OF CONTENTS

ACKNOWLEDGMENTS

Many people have helped to make this field guide possible. We thank Valerie Conley for providing technical assistance, and Alan Bessette and Sheila Orlin for reading the manuscript and making useful suggestions for improving the book. We are indebted to Outdoor Associates for permission to reproduce Barney Fowler's history of the wild boar introductions as previously reported in the *Adirondack Album, Vol. 1*. We are equally indebted to Al Lackey for clarification concerning the correct status of the bog lemming in the Adirondacks. Special thanks are due Kent Williams for sharing his expertise on cottontail rabbits. Information on reintroduction of the lynx was provided by the Adirondack Ecological Center at Newcomb. We are grateful to Philippa Brown for providing footprint illustrations, to Audrey Sherman for typesetting and making valuable suggestions for improving the manuscript, and to John Mahaffy for designing the book. We especially thank Sheila Orlin and Robert Igoe, Jr. of North Country Books for their guidance and creativity, and for giving us the opportunity to write this book.

Dennis Aprill wishes to express his appreciation to his wife, Kathleen. He also extends a personal acknowledgment to wildlife biologist, Professor John Brown.

Without the assistance of the following people this book would not exist in its present form. The majority of the photographs of medium and large mammals were taken specifically for this book within a time period of only one year. That this feat was possible was not due to the skill of the photographer, it is instead a tribute to the following network of friends. Some provided me with introductions to others on this list, who then guided me to "secret spots" from the High Peaks to Florida (for the eastern mountain lion). I am especially indebted to Valerie Conley, who accompanied me across miles, Larry Croan, Ralph E. Carman, Judy Eggleston, Carol Eiswald, Pat Grogan (who set the record for most species "found"), Tom Honig, Gordon Kirkland, David Moore, Ken Pryme, Richard Sable, Larry Watkins, Frank Webb, Al West, and Kent Williams. I also wish to single out Judy Cusworth of the Woodhaven Wildlife Center for introducing me to the fascinating world of the wildlife rehabilitators, and for permitting me to photograph several of her "charges." Other individuals who allowed me to photograph selected species are: Len Cross of Fort Rickey Game Farm, New York, and Fred Space of Space Farms, New Jersey. If I have omitted anyone else who deserves to be included, my sincere apologies. To all those who directly and indirectly assisted my photographic efforts, I once more extend my heartfelt appreciation.

—*Bill Chapman*

PHOTO CREDITS

The authors and the staff at North Country Books wish to extend their sincere appreciation to the following photographers for allowing their work to appear in this guide. We also thank all other photographers who submitted additional material for consideration. We would also like to acknowledge our debt to Joe Merrit of the Powdermill Nature Reserve in Pennsylvania, and Al Lackey, SUNY Oswego, for their assistance in securing photographs. Rodger and Joan Buttignol, John and Ann Kapcio, and Floyd Smith all provided valuable leads for securing needed photos. Sheila Orlin also invested valuable time and effort in securing quality photographs. Alan E. Bessette provided technical assistance by transforming selected photographic prints to color transparencies.

William Kent Chapman: Pl. 1, No. 2; Pl. 8, No. 3 & 4; Pl. 9, No. 2 & 4; Pl. 10, No. 1 & 4; Pl. 11, No. 4; Pl. 12, No. 2, 3 & 4; Pl. 13, No. 3; Pl. 14, No. 3, Pl. 15, No. 2, 3 & 4; Pl. 16, No. 2 & 4; Pl. 17, No. 1, 2, 3 & 4; Pl. 18, No. 3 & 4; Pl. 19, No. 3; Pl. 21, No. 1; Pl. 22, No. 2, 3 & 4; Pl. 23, No. 1, 2 & 3; Pl. 24, No. 1; Pl. 25, No. 1; Pl. 26, No. 3; Pl. 27, No. 1.

Paul Myers: Pl. 1, No. 4; Pl. 2, No. 4; Pl. 3, No. 1 & 2; Pl. 4, No. 2 & 3; Pl. 9, No. 1; Pl. 10, No. 2; Pl. 11, No. 3; Pl. 13, No. 1; Pl. 14, No. 1 & 2; Pl. 18, No. 1 & 2; Pl. 19, No. 2; Pl. 26, No. 2 & 4.

Leonard Lee Rue, III: Pl. 4, No. 4; Pl. 5, No. 4; Pl. 10, No. 3; Pl. 11, No. 2; Pl. 13, No. 4; Pl. 14, No. 4; Pl. 16, No. 1; Pl. 26, No. 1; Pl. 27, No. 3 & 4.

Monte Loomis: Cover Photo; Pl. 9, No. 3; Pl. 12, No. 1; Pl. 13, No. 2; Pl. 15, No. 1; Pl. 16, No. 3.

Alan Hicks: Pl. 6, No. 1, 2, 3 & 4; Pl. 8, No. 2; Pl. 20, No. 2.

© Merlin D. Tuttle, Bat Conservation International: Pl. 7, No. 1, 2 & 4; Pl. 8, No. 1.

Doug Pens: Pl. 7, No. 3; Pl. 19, No. 4; Pl. 20, No. 1; Pl. 27, No. 2.

Rodger W. Barbour: Pl. 1, No. 3; Pl. 2, No. 1 & 2; Pl. 3, No. 3; Pl. 4, No. 1.

Bruce Thomas: Pl. 1, No. 1; Pl. 2, No. 3; Pl. 5, No. 2

Hal S. Korber: Pl. 5, No. 1; Pl. 11, No. 1

Eric Kane, with Valerie Conley: Pl. 22, No. 1.

Zerah Cone (deceased), by permission of Rodgers Environmental Education Center: Pl. 19, No. 1.

Jeff Clarke: Pl. 20, No. 3.

John W. Pannick: Pl. 23, No. 4.

Charles H. Willey: Pl. 24, No. 2.

Milo Richmond: Pl. 3, No. 4

L. Master, The Nature Conservancy: Pl. 5, No. 3.

INTRODUCTION

This book is a field guide to those mammals found in the Adirondack area, but not restricted to it. Most of the species included here are found throughout New York State and much of the northeast. Those of us who live in the Adirondacks are indeed blessed with a virtual smorgasbord of wildlife. The mountains are a meeting place where the boreal and temperate climatic zones join, mix and coexist. Species like moose, marten and lynx are at their southern extension here, while opossum and others are at the northern limit where they can survive. Add to this the fact that there are twenty-five ecological zones and diverse habitats in the Adirondacks, and it is little wonder why the mountains are a fertile place for wildlife.

The primary objective of this field guide is to aid in the identification of unfamiliar mammals. The ability to identify mammals is especially valuable, for they often serve as natural indicators as to the status and health of the overall ecology of an area. If we compare a picture of today's Adirondacks with another made a short one hundred years ago, we find evidence of major changes. Several species have been torn from the fabric of the original panorama, while new species are being woven in. Because it is impossible to understand the Adirondacks without knowledge of all these events, we have elected to include in this guide the extirpated species, those mammals that once occurred naturally within the park but are no longer found living there.

Work on this guide included many trips through the Adirondack region. During these trips Bill Chapman conducted a very informal poll as to the status of Adirondack mammals. By a surprisingly wide margin, both residents and tourists alike believe vestige populations of wolves, panthers and wolverines still roam remote portions of the park. It was amusing to note that residents of the eastern edge located these lost colonies in the western reaches, while residents of the western area returned the favor by placing these populations in the east. This need to believe in viable populations of the larger carnivores still inhabiting the park runs very deep, and may be attributed to a romantic wish to be associated with their wildness and a desire to feel the spirit of the original Adirondacks. There may be another motivation behind those beliefs, a feeling that if we can continue to deny these species are lost, then we can also deny the fact that in every case it was our own species that inflicted the damage. One Adirondack naturalist recently made the wry observation that if we were ever judged by the same criteria we apply to those species being suggested for reintroduction, humans would likely be banned from the park, or at the very least be placed under a bounty system to control our numbers!

Few areas of nature study are as rewarding as the study of the wild mammals. This field guide has been designed to assist in the identification of all species found in the Adirondack Park, and to explain key features of their natural history. The size of this book makes it easy to carry along on hikes, camping trips and other outdoor activities. It is the authors' hope that this book will increase the reader's appreciation of the world of mammals.

ARRANGEMENT OF THE BOOK

The arrangement of this book is a continuation of traditions established by the three previous Adirondack Field Guides in this series. Information is given on the physical description, habitat, food, and reproduction of each species. Where appropriate, a section on comments gives additional information expanding on the natural history of that particular species.

As the title states, this book is a field guide and, like all field guides, its primary purpose is to help readers to identify whatever species they may encounter. To assist in this process, the mammals are divided into three major categories based on overall size. Under each of these categories are keys based on other physical characteristics that will allow the reader to complete the identification process. In the part of this book covering the small mammals, those less than ten inches in length, the natural histories of all members of each group are similar enough that they have been grouped together to avoid redundancy.

Common Name: The first information given for each mammal is its common name. This is the name that will be best known to most of the general population. It is necessary to be cautious of relying too heavily on common names. One animal may have more than one common name and, especially in the case of smaller mammals, more than one species may share the same common name.

Latin Name: Latin names are more reliable than common names for identifying all species. Each species has its own Latin name, and no two species may share that designation. Each Latin name is made up of two words. The first of these designates the genus, and indicates to what other species it may be closely related. The second word is the species designation, and this may not be shared by any other members of the same genus.

Description: The description gives vital identification characteristics such as the body size and shape, and its coloration. In many cases it will be noted that there is a difference between summer and winter coloration. If it is strikingly unique, the coloration of the young will also be described.

Habitat: Habitat is the environment where a species is most likely to be found. This can range from coniferous to deciduous forests, or from the high peaks to the valleys.

Food: Food may describe both what the animal eats and, in many cases, its feeding habits, such as the hunting strategies of selected carnivores.

Reproduction: Reproduction gives an animal's mating season, the length of its gestation period, and information on the number of young.

Comments: Comments can include any interesting or useful information not covered by the previous categories.

HOW TO USE THE KEYS

The keys scattered throughout the text are there to help the reader determine the exact identity of any mammal found within the Adirondack Park. An alternative would be to thumb through the plates until a photograph is found which closely resembles the animal in question. This can be an inefficient and frustrating approach to the identification of mammals. Therefore, use of the keys is strongly recommended.

The major key used to identify mammals starts on the next page. We will use this key to illustrate how to use all the keys in this book. Proper use will allow identification of unfamiliar specimens either down to species or at least family group. In both cases a page number will be given that will supply the reader with all additional information needed to confirm the identification.

As an example, let us say that while hiking in the Adirondacks you encounter a grayish animal with a long cylindrical, hairless tail. Turning to the key, you will see that the major sections are divided up on the basis of size; I. small, II. medium and III. large. As the animal observed is of medium size, you will consult Section II for more information. Examining Section II you will find this divided into two further choices; A., tail hairless or B., tail covered with hair. The obvious choice is to look under section A., tail hairless. Under A. you will find three choices, based on the shape of the tail and the body color of the animal. The second choice identifies a gray mammal with a cylindrical tail as an opposum, and gives a page number to turn to so you can read more about this animal. Where there is only one animal of a family present in the Adirondacks, no family key was considered necessary.

A KEY TO THE MAMMALS
OF THE ADIRONDACKS

I. **SMALL MAMMALS**, generally under 10 inches total length. This includes all rats, mice and bats. (The Norway Rat is included here even though its typical size reaches 12-18 inches because it is usually associated with the other mouse-like and rat-like species.) It is the small mammals, especially the mice and rats, which present the greatest difficulties in identification. To aid in this process, the major identification features are in bold type in this key.

A. Appearance mouse-like. **Head with an elongated, pointed snout.** Eyes and ears very small, sometimes obscured by the fur. Proportionate length of tail variable.

  1. All four feet of similar size.
     Shrews. Pages 16-19.
  2. Forefeet unusually large, shovel-shaped, and turned up at right angles. Hind feet small and of usual shape.
     Moles. Pages 20-21.

B. Appearance mouse-like. Head large, **snout blunt**, eyes and ears small. **Tail less than ½ the total length** of the combined head, body and tail measurement.

  1. Fur short, soft.
     Voles. Pages 22-25.
  2. Fur long, coarse.
     Bog Lemming. Pages 22-25.

C. Appearance mouse-like. Eyes and ears large. **Tail** about as **long** or longer than the combined head and body length, **covered with hair**.

  1. Body mouse-like, usually beautifully colored. Feet white and of normal proportions.
     White-Footed Mice. Pages 26-27.

D. Appearance mouse-like or rat-like. Eyes and ears large. **Tail** about as **long** or longer than the combined head and body length, scantily haired or hairless and

appearing scaly.
1. Body mouse-like. Total length 8-10 inches. Fore-feet small, hind feet greatly developed and unusually long.
Jumping Mice.   Pages 28-29.
2. Total length 5-8 inches. All four feet of usual proportions. Tail as long or longer than the combined head and body length.
House Mouse.   Pages 30-31.
3. Total length 12-18 inches. All four feet of usual proportions. Tail not longer than the combined head and body length.
Norway Rat.   Pages 30-32.

E. **Front limbs modified into wings**. The only true flying mammals. 8-16 inch wingspans.
Bats.   Pages 33-40.

F. The following species may be under 10 inches when first reaching maturity, but since they typically exceed this size when older, they are covered in Section II.
1. Northern Flying Squirrel.
2. Southern Flying Squirrel.
3. Eastern/Common Chipmunk.
4. Short-Tailed Weasel.

II. **MEDIUM-SIZED MAMMALS**, animals greater than 10 inches in total length and with body weight of approximately 50 pounds or less.

A. Tails hairless or nearly so.
1. Tail broad and paddle-shaped, body brown.
Beaver.   Pages 42-43.
2. Tail long, cylindrical, rat-like.
a. Body grayish white. Tail mostly flesh colored, black at the base.
Opossum.   Pages 44-45.
b. Body brown, tail dark colored. Toes partially webbed.
Muskrat.   Pages 46-47.

B. Tails covered with hair.
1. Rabbit-like animals. Hind legs longer than the front pair, modified for leaping. Eyes large, ears

long and narrow. Tail very short.
Rabbit and Hare Family.   Pages 48-52.
2. Squirrel-like animals. Bodies mostly slender, with short fur. Heads with large bright eyes, short rounded ears and long whiskers. Tail usually bushy, sometimes long.
Squirrel Family.   Pages 53-60.
3. Body distinctly dog-like, with prominent bushy tails.
Canines.   Pages 89-93.
4. Body distinctly cat-like, with short to medium (in winter) length hair. Tail short, only 4-6 inches long.
Felines.   Pages 94-97.
5. Thick-set, dark colored body covered with long hair. 2-4 inch long quills scattered throughout the hair.
Porcupine.   Pages 98-99.
6. Body stout, brownish, covered with long hair. Tail bushy, with several black bands. Face "masked."
Raccoon.   Pages 100-101.
7. Body thick-set, black with distinctive white markings. Tail bushy.
Striped Skunk (Weasel Family).   Pages 102-105.
8. Bodies long and slender. Proportionate length of tail highly variable.
Otter, fisher, marten, mink, weasel and
  ermine (Weasel Family).   Pages 102-112.

III. **LARGE MAMMALS**, animals with body weights of approximately 75-1,400 pounds.
 A. Animals with legs ending in hooves. Males with antlers.
 Deer Family   Pages 114-118.
 B. Animal with legs not ending in hooves.
  1. Body very thick-set, usually black in coloration, with very short tail. Feet with long, nonretractile claws.
  Black Bear   Pages 119-120.
  2. Body mostly hairless, slender to rotund. Colora-

tion highly variable. Walks upright on hind feet.
Man. Page 121.

IV. **EXTIRPATED MAMMALS**, species found in the Adirondack Park within the last 150 years, but have now become extinct or practically extinct there. These include the following:

Section I

Small Mammals

White-Footed Mouse
Peromyscus leucopus

SHREWS
Soricidae family

Shrews are small mouse-like animals with elongated, pointed snouts. All four feet are of a similar size. The eyes and ears are small, sometimes obscured by the fur. The proportionate length of the tail to the overall size is highly variable, and is a key identification feature.

They are extremely active, fast moving and aggressive creatures. They do not hibernate, and may be active both day and night. The short-tailed and masked shrews are probably the commonest species, followed by the water shrews. All shrews emit a musky odor that makes them unpalatable to most predators. Owls, who swallow their prey whole, are the shrews' primary enemy. There are six species known to inhabit the Adirondack Park. A seventh New York species, the least shrew (*Cryptotis parva*), is found along the entire southern border of the state. It is similar in appearance to the short-tailed shrew, but has fewer teeth and is smaller in size.

Habitat: The shrews are found in damp or moist habitats in woodlands, bogs, swamps or sometimes fields. They live in an extensive system of tunnels which may be found under layers of grass, leaf mold, sphagnum or burrowed through loose soil. They may construct the burrows themselves, or use those of other animals. They build small, spherical nests of leaves and grass for sleeping and raising their young. These nests are often located under the cover of fallen logs or old stumps.

Food: Shrews have ravenous appetites, some species consuming up to twice their body weight each day. Adult and larval insects make up the bulk of their diet. Other invertebrates are also eaten, such as centipedes, spiders, snails, slugs and worms. They have even been reported killing small mice and birds. Vegetable matter, such as seeds or fungus, is also occasionally consumed.

Reproduction: Mating takes place throughout the warmer seasons. The gestation period is 18-21 days. Up to three litters of usually 2-8 young are produced annually. The young are sexually active in a matter of months, a necessity due to their short lifespan of only 1-2 years.

KEY TO THE SHREWS

I. Tail about 25% of the total head-body length.
   A. Body gray, shorter, and snout less pointed than in other shrews, almost mole-like in appearance. Short-Tailed Shrew, *Blarina brevicauda*. Page 17.

II. Tail about 50% of the total head-body length.
   A. Body brownish. Pygmy Shrew, *Microsorex hoyi*. Page 18.

III. Tail 60-75% of the total head-body length. Body brownish.
   A. Underside of tail gray-brown. Masked Shrew, *Sorex cinereus*. Page 18.
   B. Underside of tail yellowish brown. Smoky Shrew, *Sorex fumeus*. Page 18.

IV. Tail 75-90% of the total head-body length. Body smoky to dark gray.
   A. Tail distinctly bicolored. Rear feet fringed with bristle-like hairs. Water Shrew, *Sorex palustris*. Page 19.
   B. Tail not distinctly bicolored. Rear feet lack fringe of hairs. Long-Tailed Shrew, *Sorex dispar*. Page 19.

SHORT-TAILED SHREW   Gray
Blarina brevicauda   Plate 1, No. 1

Total length: $4^{3}/_{5}$ -5 inches
Head and body: $3^{3}/_{4}$ -4 inches
Tail: 1 inch
Weight: $^{1}/_{2}$ - $^{3}/_{4}$ ounce

Description: The body is ash gray to dark gray above, somewhat paler beneath. The tail color matches the back, and is not distinctly bicolored. In winter the fur becomes a darker, leaden gray. In contrast to other Adirondack shrews, the nose and tops of the feet may be a bright pink flesh color.

Comments: The short-tailed shrew is the only Adirondack mammal having a venomous bite. It uses this trait to stun larger animals, which it then feeds on. Also known as the mole shrew.

PYGMY SHREW
Microsorex hoyi

Brown
Plate 1, No. 2

Total length: 3³/₈ inches
Head and body: 2¹/₄ inches
Tail: 1¹/₈ inches
Weight: ¹/₁₀ ounce

Description: The body is brown above, shading to gray on the underparts. The chest fur may have a reddish tinge. The tail is faintly bicolored, the upper portions the color of the back and the underside slightly paler. In winter the coat is a darker brown.

Comments: The pygmy shrew weighs only as much as a dime. It is one of the smallest, if not the smallest, mammals in the world. Also known as *Sorex hoyi*.

MASKED SHREW
Sorex cinereus

Brown
Plate 1, No. 3

Total length: 3³/₄ -4 inches
Head and body: 2¹/₄ - 2¹/₂ inches
Tail: 1¹/₄ - 1¹/₂ inches
Weight: ¹/₁₀ - ¹/₅ ounce

Description: The upper body is brown, shading to an ashy brown on the underparts and slate gray at the base. The tail is bicolored, the upper portions and around the tip the color of the upper body, the lower portions distinctly lighter. In winter the fur is a darker brown.

Comments: Also known as the common shrew. Formerly known as *Sorex personatus*.

SMOKY SHREW
Sorex fumeus

Light Brown
Plate 1, No. 4

Total length: 4¹/₄ - 4³/₄ inches
Head and body: 2¹/₂ - 2³/₄ inches
Tail: 1¹/₂ -2 inches
Weight: ²/₁₀ - ³/₁₀ ounce

Description: In summer the body is light brown above, paler beneath. In winter the body is brownish gray or slate gray above, paler beneath. The tail is bicolored, the upper portion the color of the back, the underside yellowish brown.

WATER SHREW Dark Gray
Sorex palustris Plate 2, No. 1

Total length: 5³/₄-6 inches
Head and body: 3¹/₄ - 3¹/₂ inches
Tail: 2¹/₂ - 2³/₄ inches
Weight: ¹/₃ - ⁶/₁₀ ounce

Description: The upper body is blackish gray, with gray hairs giving a frosted or hoary appearance to the fur; underparts and throat are whitish. The hind feet are adapted for swimming, with limited webbing and white fringes of bristle-like hairs. The tail is bicolored, the upper portions and around the tip is the blackish gray of the upper body, the lower portions whitish. Very little seasonal variation in the color has been reported.

Comments: Also known as the marsh or black-and-white shrew. Previously placed in the genus *Neosorex*, based on its adaptation to aquatic life.

LONG-TAILED SHREW Smoky Gray
Sorex dispar Plate 2, No. 2

Total length: 4¹/₄-5 inches
Head and body: 2¹/₂ - 2³/₄ inches
Tail: 2-2¹/₄ inches
Weight: ¹/₅ - ¹/₄ ounce

Description: The body remains smoky gray year around, sometimes slightly paler beneath. The tail is uniformly gray on both surfaces.

Comments: Also known as the rock shrew.

MOLES
Talpidae family

Moles are small mouse-like animals with elongated, pointed snouts. The forefeet are modified for burrowing, being unusually large, shovel-shaped, and turned up at right angles. The hind feet are small and of usual shape. The eyes and ears are small, sometimes obscured by the fur.

Two species inhabit the Adirondacks. A third species, the common or naked-tailed mole (*Scalopus aquaticus*) is also found in southern New York State. Although slightly larger and heavier, it generally resembles the hairy-tailed mole, except that its short tail is devoid of hair.

KEY TO THE MOLES

I. Tail short, thick, about ¼ the combined head and body length. Nose without fleshy protrubances. Hairy-tailed mole, *Parascalops breweri*. Page 21.

II. Tail long, swollen in the middle (especially in the autumn), about ¾ the combined head and body length. Nose surrounded by 22 short fleshy, finger-like protrubances. Star-nosed mole, *Condylura cristata*. Page 21.

HAIRY-TAILED MOLE
Parascalops breweri

Dark Gray
Plate 2, No. 3

Total length: 5$^1/_2$-6 inches
Head and body: 4$^1/_2$-5$^1/_4$ inches
Tail: $^9/_{10}$-1$^1/_4$ inches
Weight: 1$^1/_2$-2$^1/_4$ ounces

Description: The upper body is dark gray to near black; the underside slightly paler. The nose and feet are flesh colored. The tail is the color of the back, sometimes slightly darker.

Habitat: The hairy-tailed mole is a common underground dweller that prefers dry, sandy soil and hardwood forests.

Food: The hairy-tailed mole feeds on earthworms and insects. It has been estimated that they consume over three times their own weight of insects each day during the summer.

Reproduction: Mating takes place from March to mid-April. A gestation period of 4 weeks is followed by the birth of 4-6 young. Occasionally another litter is produced in late summer.

Comments: Also known as Brewer's mole.

STAR-NOSED MOLE
Condylura cristata

Brownish Gray
Plate 2, No. 4

Total length: 7-8 inches
Head and body: 4$^1/_4$-4$^1/_2$ inches
Tail: 3-3$^1/_4$ inches
Weight: 1$^1/_2$-2$^1/_2$ ounces

Description: The upper body is brownish black to brownish gray and the underside is paler and browner. The chin, throat, and inner thighs have a reddish tinge. The nose and feet are flesh colored. The tail is brownish gray.

Habitat: The star-nosed mole is a semi-aquatic species which prefers to live in moist or swampy areas. Inverted tunnel-like mounds of dark earth pushed up in these areas are good signs that this mole lives in the vicinity. They are strong swimmers and apparently form colonies near large bodies of water.

Food: In addition to earthworms and other terrestrial invertebrates, the star-nosed mole feeds heavily on aquatic insects.

Reproduction: Moles mate early in the year, producing a litter of 4-6 young after a gestation period of 6$^1/_2$ weeks. A second litter is sometimes produced in late summer.

VOLES AND BOG LEMMINGS
Cricetidae family

Voles and bog lemmings are small (under 8 inches total length) mouse-like animals with thick-set bodies and short limbs. The snout is blunt, and the eyes and ears are small. The tail is less than ½ the total length and covered with short hairs. The general body color is brownish above and grayish beneath.

The voles are among the commonest of the small Adirondack mammals. Bog lemmings resemble voles in general, but usually may be differentiated by their shorter tails and coarse fur. Because of strong physical similarities, the common names of mouse, vole and lemming are often used interchangably. An example of this is the bog lemming, which in only one area is known collectively as the bog-lemming, lemming-vole and lemming-mouse!

Habitat: Most voles (except for the red-backed) live in elaborate, multi-branched tunnel systems containing several nests of soft grass. These tunnels may be through dense grass, or, in the case of the woodland vole, more subterranian. Bog lemmings differ from voles in their choice of habitat. Lemmings favor bogs with heavy vegetation growth and lush beaver meadows. Because such ecological areas are scattered throughout northern New York, lemming populations are localized and vary in density from bog to bog.

Food: Voles and lemmings feed primarily on vegetation such as grasses, sedges, seeds and roots, although they will occasionally eat insects and other invertebrates.

Reproduction: Voles are known for their high reproduction rates. They will mate during any of the warm months, and after a gestation period of 17-24 days they produce a litter of 4-8 or more young. Voles are short-lived, often surviving only one year. Bog lemmings also mate during any of the warmer months. Following a gestation period of 21-23 days they produce a litter of 2-6 young.

KEY TO THE VOLES AND BOG LEMMING*

I. Tail ¼ - ⅓ of total length. Ears distinctly or partially visible. Fur short, soft.
   A. Body brown, with a distinct reddish chestnut stripe down the back. Ears distinct. Red-Backed Vole, *Clethrionomys gapperi*. Page 24.
   B. Body brown to yellow-brown. Nose brown. Ear tips just visible. Meadow Vole, *Microtus pennsylvanicus*. Page 24.
   C. Body brown to yellow-brown. Nose yellowish. Ear tips visible. Rock Vole, *Microtus chrotorrhinus*. Page 25.
II. Tail ⅕ - ¼ of total body length. Ears mostly hidden by fur.
   A. Body and upper surface of tail rusty brown. Fur short, soft. Woodland Vole, *Microtus pinetorum*. Page 25.
   B. Body and upper surface of tail brown. Fur long, coarse. Southern Bog Lemming, *Synaptomys cooperi*. Page 25.

* Although fossilized remains of the Northern Bog Lemming (*Synaptomys borealis*) have been found in the Adirondack area, a recent publication reporting the capture of this species from the High Peaks is in fact an error due to miscommunication.

RED-BACKED VOLE
Clethrionomys gapperi

Chestnut Brown
Plate 3, No. 1

Total length: 5-6 inches
Head and body: $3^3/_4$ - $4^1/_4$ inches
Tail: $1^1/_4$ - $1^3/_4$ inches
Weight: $3/_5$ - $1^1/_5$ ounces

Description: Along the back from the crown to the tail is a broad reddish chestnut stripe, interspersed with numerous black hairs. The sides are brownish to yellowish gray and the underparts, cheeks and feet are gray. The ears are chestnut-tipped. The tail is bicolored, reddish brown above with a blackish tip; underside grayish white. In winter the dorsal stripe is brighter, the rest of the body lighter and grayer. A color phase in which the grayer color is retained year around has been reported from some areas of this vole's range.

Comments: Red-backed voles prefer mature coniferous forests where there are plenty of old decaying logs with mats of moss clinging to their surfaces. They are active day and night and are good tree climbers. Formerly known as *Evotomys gapperi*.

MEADOW VOLE
Microtus pennsylvanicus

Brown
Plate 3, No. 2

Total length: $5^1/_4$ -7 inches
Head and body: $3^1/_2$ -5 inches
Tail: $1^3/_4$ - $2^1/_2$ inches
Weight: $1^1/_2$ - $2^1/_4$ ounces

Description: The color of the upper body is variable, brown to yellow-brown intermixed with black hairs, especially along the back; undersurface gray to buff. The feet are brownish. The tail is bicolored, dark brown above with an even darker tip, grayish below. In winter the fur is grayer throughout.

Comments: This common brown meadow vole prefers to live in orchards and open grassy areas of old pastures and fields.

ROCK VOLE　　　　　　　　　　Yellowish Brown
Microtus chrotorrhinus　　　　　Plate 3, No. 3

Total length: 5½-7 inches
Head and body: 4-4¾ inches
Tail: 1¾-2¼ inches
Weight: 1-1½ ounces

Description: The rock vole's body is yellowish brown above, intermixed with darker hairs. The undersurface and feet are gray. The nose is yellowish. The tail is light brown above, paler beneath.

Comments: The rock vole is easily identified by its yellow nose. This vole, as its name describes, prefers rocky, moist areas in woodlands. Also known as the yellow-nosed vole.

WOODLAND VOLE　　　　　　　　Rusty Brown
Microtus pinetorum　　　　　　　Plate 3, No. 4

Total length: 4½-5½ inches
Head and body: 2¾-4 inches
Tail: ¾-1 inch
Weight: ¾-1¼ ounces

Description: The head and body are rusty brown on the upper portions, with reddish tints. The underside and feet are gray. The upper part of the tail is rusty brown.

Comments: With its thick reddish brown fur and short tail, the woodland vole can be easily distinguished from its less colorful relatives. They are most at home in deciduous and mixed forests, but occasionally take up residence in apple orchards, damaging the bark of young fruit trees.

SOUTHERN BOG LEMMING　　　　　　Brown
Synaptomys cooperi　　　　　　　Plate 4, No. 1

Total length: 4½-5¼ inches
Head and body: 3¾-4¹/₁₀ inches
Tail: ¾-1 inch
Weight: ¾-1¼ ounces

Description: The body is brown, intermixed with light brown, gray and black hairs, creating a grizzled appearance; underparts gradually shading to light gray. The tail is brown above, whitish below.

WHITE-FOOTED MICE
Cricetidae family

The white-footed mice are among the most attractive mice. The fawn colored body contrasts beautifully with the small pure white feet. The eyes and ears are prominent. The tail is about as long or longer than the combined head and body length, and covered with hair.

Two species are included here, the white-footed mouse and the deer mouse. As the common family name suggests, they are known for their dainty, white furred feet. In winter, they form colonies to keep each other warm. Though primarily nocturnal and not often seen during daylight hours, their tiny tracks—parallel little dots in the snow—can be seen going from one clump of swale grass to another. Because they don't hibernate, are numerous and active year round, they are an important food source for weasels, foxes, owls, hawks, and snakes.

Habitat: Although these mice occur naturally in fields and woodlands, they also frequently enter human habitations. Along with chipmunks, they are common visitors in most established campsites in northern New York, but do little damage. They come to collect the crumbs that are laying around to augment their natural diet. These mice construct small nests of grass and other soft materials in which to raise their young. These nests are hidden under any available cover, ranging from fallen timber to old buildings.

Food: The white-footed mice are omniverous feeders, consuming seeds, fruit, fungi, even insects and other invertebrates. One of their favorite foods is wild cherry pits, which they store in tree cavities for winter use.

Reproduction: They are promiscuous breeders, mating during any and all of the warmer months. A litter of 4-7 or more young is born after a gestation period of about 23 days.

KEY TO THE WHITE-FOOTED MICE

The following easily observable characteristics are highly variable in both species, making identification based on this key probable but not definitive. Of the two, the white-footed mouse is a more southern species and likely to be more plentiful in the Lake Champlain and Lake George basins.

I. Tail shorter than combined head-body length. Body reddish brown above, cream beneath. Tail not white-tipped. White-Footed Mouse, *Peromyscus leucopus*. Page 27.

II. Tail equal to or slightly longer than the combined head-body length. Body grayish brown above, pure white beneath. Tail white-tipped. Deer Mouse, *Peromyscus maniculatus*. Page 27.

WHITE-FOOTED MOUSE Brownish Fawn
Peromyscus leucopus Plate 4, No. 2 & 4

Total length: 6-7³/₄ inches
Head and body: 3¹/₅ - 4¹/₄ inches
Tail: 2⁴/₅ - 3¹/₂ inches
Weight: ²/₃ - 1 ounce

Description: The body and cheeks are brownish fawn, darkest on the back where the fur intermixes with many black hairs. The throat and underside are cream white. The feet are white. The tail is brownish above, cream below. In winter the fur becomes longer, thicker, bright golden fawn above and white beneath.

DEER MOUSE Grayish Brown
Peromyscus maniculatus Plate 4, No. 3

Total length: 5-8 inches
Head and body: 2¹/₂ -4 inches
Tail: 2¹/₂ -4 inches
Weight: ²/₃ - 1 ounce

Description: The body and cheeks are grayish brown, somewhat darker along the back. The throat and undersides are pure white. The feet are white. The tail is distinctly bicolored, brownish above, white beneath, and white-tipped.

JUMPING MICE
Zapodidae family

The jumping mice are among the easiest of the small mouse-like mammals to identify. The combination of a very long tail —much longer than the combined head and body length—and the unusually large hind feet clearly differentiate them from all other species.

One way to tell if meadow jumping mice are in the neighborhood is to walk through a grassy meadow early in the morning after an evening with heavy dew. Invariably, if meadow jumping mice are nearby, they will make a three-foot diagonal jump. With the dew glistening on their bodies, they may at first appear to be large unusual insects. These mice usually make one leap, then wait, so the observer may initially hear the faint thump in the underbrush as the animal lands.

Habitat: Two species of jumping mice call the Adirondacks home, the meadow jumping mouse and the woodland jumping mouse. Both are aptly named. Woodland jumping mice prefer to live in remote deciduous forests while the meadow jumping mouse may be found in beaver meadows, old pastures and logging clear cuts, especially if a stream or pond is nearby. Unlike its woodland relation, the meadow jumping mouse is often found near human populations. Jumping mice dig small burrows, in which they pass the winter in leafy nests. Both are true hibernators, so their tracks will not be seen in winter.

Food: Jumping mice are omniverous, living on a varied diet of seeds, berries, small nuts, insects and fungi.

Reproduction: Mating occurs during the warmer months, resulting in 2-3 litters a year. Four to six or more young are born in each litter after a gestation period of 18-25 days.

KEY TO THE JUMPING MICE

I. Sides of body yellowish, with a broad, sharply defined brown band down the back. Tail white-tipped. Woodland Jumping Mouse, *Napaeozapus insignis*. Page 29.

II. Sides of body brownish yellow. Back darker, but without distinct color borders. Tail not white-tipped. Meadow Jumping Mouse, *Zapus hudsonius*. Page 29.

WOODLAND JUMPING MOUSE
Napaeozapus insignis

Brown above
Yellowish sides
Plate 5, No. 1

Total length: 8-10 inches
Head and body: 3½-4 inches
Tail: 4½-6 inches
Weight: ½-1 ounce

Description: The sides of the body and the cheeks are yellowish intermixed with some brown hairs. From the nose and crown down the back runs a sharply defined band, brown intermixed with some yellow hairs. The breast and underparts are white. The tail is white-tipped and bicolored, the upper parts the color of the back, the underside white.

MEADOW JUMPING MOUSE
Zapus hudsonius

Brownish Yellow
Plate 5, No. 2

Total length: 7½-9 inches
Head and body: 3-3¼ inches
Tail: 4¼-5¾ inches
Weight: ½-1 ounce

Description: The sides are brownish yellow, intermixed with darker hairs, especially along the back. The underparts are buffy white. The tail is bicolored, dusky brown above and buffy white below. The fur is paler and yellower in winter.

Comments: Formerly known as *Dipus hudsonius*.

OLD WORLD RATS AND MICE
Muridae family

In appearance, these old world introductions are typically mouse-like or rat-like in outline. The tail is long, about as long as the combined head and body length, and appears scaly. The eyes and ears are very prominent. Both the rat and the house mouse originated in Eurasia. Sometime in the past they became dependent upon mankind for both food and shelter. Since then they have followed humans throughout the world, probably arriving in North America with the Hessian mercenaries during the American Revolution. Norway rats are capable of carrying murine typhus, bubonic plague and salmonellosis. This, combined with the damage they inflict on food stores and habitations, has earned them the wrath of humankind. Ironically, albino forms of both of these species are used in laboratory research aimed at eliminating disease. Their primary enemies in the Adirondacks, besides humans, are barn owls and great horned owls, although hawks, snakes and other predators will also kill rats.

In southeastern New York a third introduction, the black rat (*Rattus rattus*) is found. In size it is very similar to the Norway rat, but its build is more slender and its tail is longer than its combined head-body length. The roof rat of the same area is only a distinct variety of the black rat species.

Another southeastern New York species sometimes confused with the Norway rat is the woodrat (*Neotoma floridana*). This is a native species, and despite its common name it is more closely related to the white-footed mice than to the true rats. In color, size and tail-body ratio it is similar to the Norway rat, but it may be distinguished by its whiter underparts and by having a furry, not scaly-appearing tail. The woodrat is an inoffensive woodland resident, more deserving of protection than the persecution that is directed at the true old world rats and mice.

Habitat: The Norway rat and house mouse are now found in the Adirondacks in both towns and farming areas. In towns, they inhabit old buildings and are commonly found in dumps. When they live in farming areas, rats will often migrate to grain fields during the warmer months and return indoors when the weather turns cold. The house mouse and the rat can exist in northern New York only because of the presence of people. Both species raise their young in nests made of soft materials such as grass or paper.

Food: These species will feed on almost anything from plant to animal matter, with no regard to the age or condition of the meal. Rats are also ferocious gnawers that will chew through (and even consume!) almost anything, including aluminum electric cable, concrete, wood, even books and other paper products.

Reproduction: Both of these species mate year around. Following a gestation period of 20-22 days, they produce a litter of 5-10 young. They are highly prolific, and capable of producing 5-10 or more litters a year!

KEY TO THE OLD WORLD RATS AND MICE

  I. Total length 5-8 inches. Tail almost as long and sometimes longer than the combined head-body length. House Mouse, *Mus musculus*. Page 31.

  II. Total length 12-18 inches. Tail not longer than the combined head-body length. Norway Rat, *Rattus norvegicus*. Page 32.

HOUSE MOUSE   Gray-Brown
Mus musculus   Plate 5, No. 3

Total length: 5-8 inches
Head and body: $3\frac{1}{4}$-4 inches
Tail: $2\frac{2}{3}$-$3\frac{1}{2}$ inches
Weight: $\frac{1}{2}$-$\frac{4}{5}$ ounce

Description: The body is a grayish brown, darkest along the back. The face and shoulders are tinged with yellowish brown. Underparts are grayish, sometimes with a reddish brown tint. The tail is dusky brown.

NORWAY RAT
Rattus norvegicus

Gray-Brown
Plate 5, No. 4

Total length: 12-18 inches
Head and body: 6½-9 inches
Tail: 6-8½ inches
Weight: 10-15 ounces

Description: The back of the body is rusty to a yellow grayish brown, with an intermixing of long black hairs. It is grayer on the sides becoming grayish-white on the underparts. The ears are dull brown. The tail is dusky gray above, paler beneath.

Comments: Formerly known as *Mus norvegicus*.

BATS
Vespertilionidae family

The bats may be the easiest of all the Adirondack mammal groups to identify. They have small mouse-like bodies which are covered with soft fur. Their most distinctive feature is that the front limbs have evolved into wings which range from 8 to 16 inches wide, depending on the species.

All bats are members of the order *Chiroptera*. Four families of bats occur within the United States, the *Mormoopidae*, *Phyllostomatidae*, *Vespertilionidae*, and the *Molossidae*. Collectively, they account for 39 species of bats known to inhabit this country. Nine species of bats have been found in the Adirondacks, all members of the *Vespertilionidae* family, the evening bats. Of all these species, only the little brown bat, *Myotis lucifigus*, is truly common throughout this area. The others range from rare to uncommon to locally abundant near colony locations. Only two other species not found in the Adirondacks have been reported elsewhere in New York State. A seminole bat, *Lasiurus seminolus*, was found in Ithaca, and there is a report of the evening bat, *Nycticeius humeralis*, in extreme western New York.

Habitat: During the day bats roost in the dark quiet places that are associated with their kind, such as caves, hollow trees or empty buildings. Two of our largest bats, the hoary bat and the red bat, do not spend their days in such confined quarters. Instead, they hang upside down in semi-shade on branches of trees, usually overlooked even when they are observed, for in this state they appear as dead and shrivelled leaves. Three of our bats, the hoary bat, the red bat and silver-haired bat, migrate south before winter arrives. At least some members of the remaining six species spend their winters hibernating in deep caves or other protected locations.

Food: All Adirondack bats depend on flying insects for food. They are most commonly observed when feeding near trees, along the edge of woodlots, over waterways or around outdoor lights, all prime areas to find high concentrations of insects.

Reproduction: The reproductive habits are interesting. Most mating takes place in the autumn, some in the spring and occasionally during warm spells that break the winter hibernation period. Depending on the species, young may be born from late May into July. This observation led to the belief that a bat's gestation period could be as long as nine or ten months. It has since been learned that female bats have the ability to store viable sperm in their bodies, so that a female who mated in September may not actually become pregnant until the following spring. Gestation periods run from 45 to 90 days, with the smaller species usually having the shortest gestations and the largest species the longest.

All of our bats, except the hoary and red bats, have only two mammary glands. The hoary and the red bat each have four, so it is not surprising that these two species sometimes give birth to litters of three or four. The other species usually give birth in litters of one or more often two, except for the four species of the *Myotis* genera, which typically give birth to only one young at a time. These small brown bats bear their young in June and July, the other species giving birth late May through June. In all species the young are usually ready to fly in three to four weeks.

A KEY TO THE BATS

I. Interfemoral membrane hairless or only sparsely haired near the base. (The interfemoral membrane is the winglike webbing connecting the hind feet with the tail.) These species have two mammary glands.
   A. Fur brown, sometimes glossy. Back hairs usually bicolored. Wingspans 8-10 inches.
      1. Body glossy brown. Little Brown Bat, *Myotis lucifugus*. Page 36.
      2. Body yellow-brown. Keen's Myotis, *Myotis septentrionalis*. Page 36.
      3. Body dull brown. Indiana Bat, *Myotis sodalis*. Page 37.
      4. Body golden brown. Small-Footed Bat, *Myotis leibii*. Page 37.
   B. Fur black, with silvery white tips. Wingspan 10-12 inches.
      1. Silver-Haired Bat, *Lasionycteris noctivagans*. Page 38.
   C. Fur light yellowish brown. Hairs with three color bands. Wingspan 8-10 inches.
      1. Eastern Pipistrelle, *Pipistrellus subflavus*. Page 38.
   D. Fur dark, glossy brown. Hairs bicolored. Wingspan 12-13 inches.
      1. Big Brown Bat, *Eptesicus fuscus*. Page 39.
II. Interfemoral membrane covered with fur on the upper side. Both species have four mammary glands.
   A. Back hairs have four color zones. Wingspan 11-16 inches.
      1. Body rufous (reddish). Red Bat, *Lasiurus borealis*. Page 39.
      2. Body brown. Hoary Bat, *Lasiurus cinereus*. Page 40.

LITTLE BROWN BAT
Myotis lucifugus

Glossy Brown
Plate 6, No. 1

Wingspan: 8-10 inches
Length: 3-3³/₄ inches
Tail: 1¹/₄ - 1¹/₂ inches
Weight: ¹/₄ - ¹/₂ ounce

Description: The body is glossy yellow-brown above, buff below. Back hairs are bicolored, with dark brown bases and light brown above. There is often a darker spot on the shoulders in front of the wings. Wing membranes a dark glossy brown.

Comments: The little brown is the most common bat in the Adirondacks and can be found in buildings and trees. During June, July and August, they can be seen flying about street lights which often attract throngs of insects. Although they have 8-inch wingspans, when their wings are folded in little browns are small enough to enter homes through tiny foundation and attic openings. In the fall, they will hibernate in caves and old mineshafts. While in hibernation in a moist cave, the dew that forms on the little brown bat's fur and its deep sleep gives the animal a look of being in suspended animation.

KEEN'S MYOTIS
Myotis septentrionalis

Yellow-Brown
Plate 6, No. 2

Wingspan: 9-10¹/₂ inches
Length: 3-3¹/₂ inches
Tail: 1¹/₄ - 1¹/₂ inches
Weight: ¹/₄ - ³/₁₀ ounce

Description: The body light yellow to reddish brown, paler beneath. Back hairs are bicolored, with very dark bases and yellow to reddish brown above. Wing membranes are dark brown.

Comments: Up until the late 1980's it was thought that the Keen's myotis from the east and west coasts were one species, designated as *Myotis keenii*. It is now believed that the east coast bats are a separate species, currently listed as *Myotis septentrionalis*. To avoid further confusion it has been suggested that the eastern group be given the common name of either northern long-eared bat or northern myotis.

INDIANA BAT
Brown
Myotis sodalis
Plate 6, No. 3

Wingspan: 9-10 inches
Length: 2³/₄ - 3¹/₂ inches
Tail: 1¹/₄ - 1³/₄ inches
Weight: about ¹/₄ ounce

Description: The Indiana bat's body is dull gray brown to dark brown above, slightly grayer beneath. Back hairs are tricolored; very dark at the base, gray above and brown-tipped. The nose and lips are pinkish brown. Wing membranes are dark brown.

Comments: The Indiana bat resembles the little brown and, like the little brown, is a cave bat needing a controlled environment for hibernation. When such a cave or mineshaft is found, Indiana bats will pack themselves tightly together in roosting positions to sleep the winter away. They are probably the most social of northern New York bats. It is on the Endangered Species List.

SMALL-FOOTED BAT
Golden Brown
Myotis leibii
Plate 6, No. 4

Wingspan: 8-9¹/₂ inches
Length: 2³/₄ - 3¹/₄ inches
Tail: 1¹/₄ - 1¹/₂ inches
Weight: about ¹/₄ ounce

Description: The body is golden brown and the back hairs are bicolored, very dark at the base, brown above. The face and ears are black. Wing membranes are very dark brown.

Comments: The small-footed is a locally abundant bat with an identifiable dark face mask to compliment its yellowish brown fur. Like little brown bats, they overwinter in caves and mineshafts. In summer, small-footed bats prefer coniferous forests where they fly about the understory in search of insects.

SILVER-HAIRED BAT
Lasionycteris noctivagans

Frosted Black
Plate 7, No. 1

Wingspan: 10-12 inches
Length: 3$\frac{1}{2}$-4 inches
Tail: 1$\frac{1}{2}$-1$\frac{3}{4}$ inches
Weight: $\frac{1}{4}$-$\frac{1}{3}$ ounce

Description: The silver-haired bat's body is very dark brown or black on both upper and lower surfaces. The hairs are silver-tipped, giving the back (more than the belly) a frosted appearance, especially in younger specimens. The head, throat and wing membranes are blackish.

Comments: Silver-haired bats favor wet areas such as ponds and rivers to search out flies and beetles. In the fall, the silver-haired bat migrates to the southeastern states to find a suitable tree cavity or underbark in which to pass the winter season.

EASTERN PIPISTRELLE
Pipistrellus subflavus

Yellow-Brown
Plate 7, No. 2

Wingspan: 8-10 inches
Length: 3-3$\frac{1}{2}$ inches
Tail: 1$\frac{1}{4}$-1$\frac{3}{4}$ inches
Weight: $\frac{1}{8}$-$\frac{1}{4}$ ounce

Description: The body is gray-brown to dark yellow-brown on the upper surface, a lighter yellow-brown on the lower. The back hairs exhibit three colors, gray at the base, yellow- brown in the middle, and brown at the tip. The wing membranes are blackish.

Comments: The eastern pipistrelle gets its name from the Latin *pipilo* meaning to squeak or chatter. This is an appropriate name for the small bat that chatters about the evening sky while consuming almost one quarter of its weight in insects in less than a half hour. They are cave bats and need the relatively constant temperature and moist surroundings provided by caves and mineshafts to hibernate. In late May, the pipistrelle's internal clock wakes it for yet another season of insect gathering.

BIG BROWN BAT
Eptesicus fuscus

Brown
Plate 7, No. 3

Wingspan: 12-13 inches
Length: 4-5 inches
Tail: 1½-2 inches
Weight: about ½ ounce

Description: The body is dark to dusky brown on the back, lighter and grayer below. The back hairs are bicolored, black at the base and brown on the upper portions. The face, ears and wing membranes are blackish.

Comments: The big brown can only be called large when compared with the little brown, and since both bats rarely fly together such a comparison may not be possible for the average observer. The big brown's wingspan is about 12 inches (robin size). A fairly common species, it is one of the fastest and hardiest of Adirondack bats. Big browns can be seen flying about as late as November, particularly if there is a late hatch of beetles or flies. Although many big browns migrate long distances to caves, some overwinter in walls and attics.

RED BAT
Lasiurus borealis

Rusty Red
Plate 7, No. 4

Wingspan: 11-12¾ inches
Length: 3¾-4¾ inches
Tail: 1¾-2¼ inches
Weight: ⅓-½ ounce

Description: The body of females ranges from dark rufous to rusty red, the underside is a paler fawn color. Coloration on the males is lighter and brighter, from yellowish red to dull orange above and a paler buff color beneath. Both sexes have white-tipped hairs, but this trait is most noticeable on the back of the female. The back hairs have black bases, yellow then red in the middle, and are white-tipped. There is a white patch on the shoulder in front of each wing. The wing membranes are brownish black.

Comments: The red is one of the easiest of Adirondack bats to identify because its bright coloring can often be noticed as the animal flies the evening sky in search of insects. It is a tree bat, preferring to hibernate in tree cavities where the winter temperature is more variable. In fact, temperature variations are essential to sleeping tree bats, particularly in early spring when the warmer temperatures provide the impetus to awaken. In a temperature controlled cave, tree bats would perish, dying of starvation while they slept. As its Latin name *Borealis* (meaning north) indicates, this very hardy bat can be found throughout the northeast and well into Canada. Red bats are even hardier than big browns and have been observed roosting in the open while they are covered with snow.

HOARY BAT
Frosted Brown

Lasiurus cinereus
Plate 8, No. 1

Wingspan: 14-16 inches
Length: 5-5½ inches
Tail: 2-2¼ inches
Weight: ¾ - 1½ ounces

Description: The hoary bat's body is dark brown to deep yellow-brown, with many white-tipped hairs, giving this bat a frosted or "hoary" appearance. The underside is paler, and also frosted. The back hairs have nearly black bases, creamy yellow then dark brown zones, and are white-tipped. The head is brown, with black on the muzzle, around each eye and on the edges of the ears. There is a white patch on each shoulder in front of the wing, and a broad yellow band across the throat. The wing membranes are brownish black.

Comments: With a wing span up to 16 inches, the hoary is the largest bat in the Adirondacks. It is also the least common. Its flight pattern is characterized by short glides as it seeks out moths, dragonflies and other large insects. The hoary bat seems to prefer conifer forests to breed. It migrates to the deep south in late fall.

Section II

Medium-Sized Mammals

Short-Tailed Weasel
Mustela erminea

BEAVER
Castoridae family

The beaver is the state mammal of New York. Almost extinct at the turn of the century, protection and restocking have led to a current population explosion. When beavers colonize a new area, they first dam up a stream, flooding and killing trees in the backwater. At times these dams affect land already in use by man, putting them into conflict with local human populations. After constructing their lodges, beavers begin to enjoy the lush food supply available. Unfortunately, they have a tendency to overcut the surrounding trees and after a year or two are forced to travel inland for food. Finally, after all available food is utilized, the beavers will move on. The dam collapses and eventually the site will be reclaimed by grasses, wildflowers, and then saplings. This entire process takes years, and with each change in habitat comes a different group of animals and birds. Thus, the beaver is constantly altering the Adirondack landscape.

BEAVER
Castor canadensis

Glossy Brown
Plate 8, No 3 & 4
Plate 25, No. 1

Total length: 34-45 inches
Head and body: 25-35 inches
Tail: 11-18 inches
Weight: 30-50 pounds

Description: The beaver has a large, thick and heavy body. The head is broad and rounded, with short, rounded ears. The forefeet are small. The hind feet, adapted for swimming, are broad and webbed and are unique by usually having a double claw on the second toe. The tail is broad, horizontally flat, and scaly.

In summer the body is dark red-brown, the longest hairs tipped with glossy chestnut. The lighter reddish tinges are most pronounced on the head and the rump. The ears and tail are black. The feet and undersurface are chocolate/seal brown. In winter the body is darker, becoming blackish brown.

Habitat: Beavers are invariably found near large bodies of water with timbered shorelines. They will dig tunnels for dens in areas of fast running water, or construct the familiar dams and lodges in slow moving or standing water. Their lodges are large, hollow, dome-shaped structures built of small trees and branches cemented with mud.

Food: They feed on tender shoots and roots of aquatic plants in the warmer months, and various kinds of bark (cottonwood, aspen, willow, alder, birch and even evergreen) in winter. A supply of these foods are cached under water near the den for winter feedings. Sharp teeth set in massive jaws allow the beavers to bite through living trees.

Reproduction: The mating season lasts from January through March, peaking in February. The gestation period lasts about 112 days. A single litter averaging 4-5 young is born in May or June.

OPOSSUM
Didelphidae family

The opposum is the only North American marsupial—a species whose young are born prematurely and protected in the female's fur-lined pouch. It is often thought of as a more southern species, and the Adirondacks are close to their northern range limit. Even though it is expanding its range northward, the opossum in northern New York is probably confined to the southern Adirondacks and Champlain Valley, though occasionally one will be seen in cities further to the north.

Although they are slow moving and have a small brain, they have survived nearly unchanged for over 70 million years, outlasting the dinosaurs and the great Cretaceous extinctions. Primarily nocturnal, they can occasionally be seen lumbering about during the early mornings and evenings in the spring and summer. When startled, opossums don't always "play possum" by rolling on their backs, but usually hurry to safety in lieu of feigning death.

OPOSSUM　　　　　　　　　　　　　Grizzled Gray
Didelphis virginiana　　　　　　　　Plate 9, No. 1 & 2

Total length: 22-34 inches
Head and body: 15-20 inches
Tail: 9-15 inches
Weight: 5-12 pounds

Description: The opossum may be recognized by its grizzled gray color, medium-size, head with a long pointed muzzle, beadlike black eyes, hairless ears and long hairless and scaly tail. These features combine to give it a rat-like appearance.

Body grayish white, intermixed with white and black-tipped hairs. Throat and underparts white. Face white with a pink nose, ears black with white tips. Legs brownish black, upper surface of the feet dirty white. Tail black at the base, dull flesh colored the rest of its length. The tail is long and prehensile, (adapted for grasping or seizing), and can be used as a fifth limb during climbing.

Habitat: The opossum usually lives in wooded areas bordered by human habitations. They seem especially fond of farmlands and orchards.

Food: They are omnivorous, eating insects, wild fruits and nuts, crayfish, carrion, eggs and small rodents. They occasionally raid farmyards for poultry, apples or corn.

Reproduction: A first mating season occurs in late winter, a second season occurs in May-June, and sometimes there is even a third mating later in the year. The gestation period is 13 days. Six or more young are born per litter. They remain in the pouch about two months.

MUSKRAT
Cricetidae family

The muskrat is common throughout the Adirondack wetlands of northern New York. Its greatest population densities are found in the marshy areas near St. Regis Falls, Lake Champlain and Lake George.

It has a long, hairless tail that acts as a rudder. In snow or mud, the rope-like imprint of the muskrat's tail drag is almost always visible.

MUSKRAT   Dark Brown
Ondatra zibethicus   Plate 9, No. 3 & 4

Total length: 21-25 inches
Head and body: 11-13 inches
Tail: 10-12 inches
Weight: 2-3 1/2 pounds

Description: Muskrats are medium-sized, rat-like animals. The body is thick-set, with short legs. The forefeet are small. The hind feet, adapted for swimming, are large, broad and partially webbed. The ears are small and barely visible. The tail is long, scaly, rounded and slightly flattened laterally.

Body chestnut brown to dark brown, darkest on the crown and back. The body becomes paler on the sides, gradually fading to gray on the undersides. The ground color is intermixed with longer glossy hairs of a darker brown color both above and beneath. The cheeks are gray, the throat and lips are white and the chin is white with a blackish spot. The feet are dark brown, the tail is almost black. There is little seasonal variation in color.

Habitat: Muskrat colonies can be found along bodies of water of all sizes in the Adirondacks, especially if there is a good supply of cattails and other aquatic plants nearby. Like beavers, muskrats build dome-shaped homes in marshes, but muskrat lodges are smaller and are composed of cattails, sedges and other marsh plants. Along streams, they often den in holes that begin below the water line then gradually rise to a dry platform a few feet further inland.

Food: Muskrats feed on the roots and shoots of cattails and other plants that live in or near water.

Reproduction: Breeding begins with the first warmings of spring and peaks in late spring or early summer. It is not unusual for additional matings to occur through early autumn. The gestation period lasts about 28 days. Up to 5 litters averaging 6 young apiece are born each year.

RABBIT AND HARE FAMILY
Leporidae family

Rabbits and hares are medium-sized animals which are covered with extremely soft fur. (The only exception to this generalization is the kinky-haired European Hare.) The nose is blunt, eyes large, ears long and narrow. The hind legs are much longer than the front pair, and modified for leaping. The tail is short, upturned when running, exposing the white underside.

Of the four members of this family that have inhabited New York State, three are native and one was introduced. All three of the native species, the eastern and New England cottontails and the snowshoe hare, are currently found within the Adirondack Park. Earlier in this century sportman's clubs attempted to introduce additional species; the European hare, *Lepus europeaus*, and possibly also the black-tailed jackrabbit, *Lepus californicus*. Of these, the European hare was most widely stocked, but this species did not do well in the Adirondacks, and it is questionable whether or not any vestige populations still exist here.

KEY TO THE RABBIT AND HARE FAMILY

I. Hind foot 4½-5½ inches long. Toes may be widely spread. Total length 17-27 inches. The true hares.
   A. Total length 17-19 inches. Rear toes widely spread. Hair straight. White in winter. Snowshoe Rabbit, *Lepus americanus*. Page 49.
   B. Total length 25-27 inches. Rear toes not widely spread. Hair kinky. Not white in winter. European Hare, *Lepus europaeus*. Page 50.

II. Hind foot 3-4 inches long. Toes not widely spread. Total length 16-18 inches. The cottontails.
   A. Ears usually bordered in dusky brown. Area between the ears brown. Often a white patch on the forehead. Eastern Cottontail, *Sylvilagus floridanus*. Page 51.
   B. Ears usually bordered in black. Area between the ears black. No white patch on the forehead. New England Cottontail, *Sylvilagus transitionalis*. Page 52.

SNOWSHOE RABBIT
Lepus americanus

Total length: 17-19 inches
Tail: 1½-2 inches
Weight: 2-4 pounds

Summer: Light Brown
Winter: White
Plate 10, No. 1 & 2

Description: In summer the upper body is light brown to rusty brown, with an intermixing of black-tipped hairs, especially along the back. The underparts are white. The ears are bordered with white hairs, and black-tipped. The tail is blackish gray above, white underneath. In winter this rabbit appears white all over, except for the eyes and the black tips on the ears, which remain dark year around. During the color-changing molt, which takes place in late spring and again in fall, intermediate stages may be observed, such as a brown body with white legs and feet.

Habitat: The snowshoe typically inhabits coniferous woods, tamarack or Arbor Vitae swamps, and willow thickets. It does not typically inhabit burrows, although it sometimes seeks shelter in larger caves.

Food: The snowshoe eats a variety of foods including grasses, shoots and leaves in summer; in winter they survive on a diet of buds, bark (poplar, willow, yellow birch) and berry canes. Since they eat much the same food as deer, there can be some confusion as to which species is browsing a certain area, especially if there is no snow on the ground to show the tracks. One sure way to tell the difference is to observe the ends of the branches: deer rip off the twigs and stems leaving a ragged branch, while hares neatly prune at almost perfect 45° angles.

Reproduction: They mate from April through June. Their gestation period runs about 36 days. Two to three litters of 2-4 young are born from May through July. The young are born in sheltered nests of grass. Snowshoes are completely furred when born. This is in contrast to the cottontails, which bear hairless offspring.

Comments: The feet of the snowshoe rabbit are disproportionately large with widely spread, well-furred toes. These function as natural snowshoes allowing this rabbit to travel across snow that would not otherwise support its weight. The most common sign is their tracks in the snow. The tracks form a crude triangle with the front two prints parallel and the back feet close together at the triangle apex. These sets of tracks may be ten feet or more apart. Because snowshoes follow pretty much the same runways all winter, they will leave well worn trails throughout snow covered underbrush.

In the far north of Canada, snowshoes go through cycles of population increases and declines, but such dramatic population changes have not been recorded in the Adirondacks. There may be some population fluctuations locally, but these do not seem to have the tremendous impact on wildlife they do further to the north. This is a good thing for the coyote, fox, bobcat, lynx, fisher, owl and hawk who utilize the snowshoe as an important food source.

Although best known in the Adirondacks as the snowshoe rabbit, this species is actually a true hare, and in some localities is referred to as the snowshoe hare or varying hare.

EUROPEAN HARE
Lepus europaeus

Light Brown
Plate 10, No. 3

Total length: 25-27 inches
Tail: $2^3/4$ - $3^3/4$ inches
Weight: 7-12 pounds

Description: The body is light brown to yellowish brown, intermixed with black hairs; the underparts are white. The ear tips are black. The top of tail is black, white beneath. Its color is paler in winter. The hair is unusually kinky.

Habitat: The European hare prefers to live in open fields.

Food: Preferred foods include grasses and small fruits.

Reproduction: Like other members of the rabbit family, it has several litters of young during the warmer months. There are 3-4 young in each litter.

Comments: It is a much larger animal than our native snowshoe. It is also listed as *Lepus capensis*.

THE COTTONTAILS

Two species of cottontail rabbit have been found in the Adirondack Park. Of the two, the eastern cottontail is by far the more common. There is individual variability in the coloration of both species, making identifications by field characteristics difficult at times, although the two are easily differentiated if the skulls are available for examination.

Habitat: Cottontail rabbits are found in woodlots, bushy areas and in fields. Although they often seek shelter in burrows, they are burrows built by other animals. Cottontails build small nests lined with soft grass and body fur in which to bear their young.

Food: Its diet is comprised mainly of shoots and leaves during the growing season; in winter they survive by consuming buds and barks such as sumac and blackberry.

Reproduction: They will mate during any of the warm months. The gestation period runs about 28 days. Several litters of 4-5 or more young are born throughout the warm months.

EASTERN COTTONTAIL
Sylvilagus floridanus

Total length: 16-18 inches
Tail: 1½-2 inches
Weight: 2-3¼ pounds

Variegated Browns
Plate 10, No. 4
Plate 11, No. 1 & 2

Description: The body hair is an intermixing of brown, cinnamon, russet, and gray, which is especially pronounced towards the rump. The nape is reddish brown. The underparts are white, with a brown band across the breast. The eyes are surrounded by a small ring of buff-colored hairs, and there is often a white patch on the forehead. The ears are usually bordered in dusky brown, becoming darker towards the tips. The upper surface of the tail is colored like the back, the undersurface is the cotton white that gives this rabbit its common name.

NEW ENGLAND COTTONTAIL　　Variegated Browns
Sylvilagus transitionalis　　Plate 11, No. 3 & 4

Total length: 16-18 inches
Tail: 1½-2 inches
Weight: 2-3¼ pounds

Description: The body hairs are various shades of brown, intermixed with black hairs, especially along the back. The underparts are white, with a brown band across the breast. The eyes are surrounded by a small ring of buff-colored hairs. The ears are bordered in black, with a distinct black patch between them. The upper surface of the tail is colored like the back, the undersurface is cotton white.

Comment: Also known as the northern cottontail.

SQUIRREL FAMILY
Sciuridae family

There are six members of the squirrel family found in the Adirondacks, including the well-known gray and red squirrels, two species of rarely seen flying squirrels, the comical chipmunk and the stocky woodchuck. Squirrels are well known for their large bright eyes, short rounded ears and long whiskers. They have unusually bushy tails. With the exception of the somewhat stout woodchuck, squirrels tend to have slender bodies. The toes have large claws for climbing or burrowing.

Most members of the squirrel family live in trees, although the woodchuck and the chipmunk may be found in burrows. Most squirrels remain active all winter. The best known exception is the hibernating woodchuck, whose first appearance is a sure sign that spring has arrived. The little chipmunk also passes part of the winter in a state of near hibernation.

The fox squirrel, *Sciurus niger*, inhabits western New York, but does not occur in or near the Park. It is a large squirrel, with 20-25 inches total length (about half of which is tail) and weighing 1½ - 2½ pounds. Its general color is gray, but this is often intermixed with many yellowish brown hairs.

KEY TO THE SQUIRREL FAMILY

A. Body stout, 20-25 inches total length, color generally brown. Ground dwelling. Woodchuck, *Marmota monax*. Page 54.

B. Body slender. Often observed in trees. Tail about 50% total length. 17-20 inches total length. Color generally gray. Gray Squirrel, *Sciurus carolinensis*. Page 56.

C. Body slender. Often observed in trees. Tail about 40% total length.
   1. 11-13 inches total length. Body reddish brown. Red Squirrel, *Tamiasciurus hudsonicus*. Page 57.
   2. 8-10 inches total length. Chestnut red, handsomely marked with horizontal black stripes. Eastern/Common Chipmunk, *Tamias striatus*. Page 58.
   3. 8½-12 inches total length. Brown to grayish brown. A loose fold of skin connecting the feet may be spread into a gliding membrane. Flying Squirrel.
      a. Belly fur pure white. Southern Flying Squirrel, *Glaucomys volans*. Page 59.
      b. Belly fur gray with white tips. Northern Flying Squirrel, *Glaucomys sabrinus*. Page 60.

WOODCHUCK   Light Brown
Marmota monax   Plate 12, No. 1

Total length: 20-25 inches
Head and body: 16-19 inches
Tail: 4-7 inches
Weight: 6-10 pounds

Description: The color of the body is variable, ranging from light brown to yellowish brown, prominently variegated by numerous white-tipped hairs. The top of the head is dark brown, the cheeks and sides of the muzzle are often marked with gray. The underparts are paler, and especially near the limbs, tinged with rusty brown. The tail and the feet are dark brown to black. All black or nearly black specimens are not uncommon.

Habitat: In the Adirondacks, woodchucks are common roadside and pastureland dwellers, not animals of the deep wilderness. It is doubtful that they were plentiful in the mountains before the clearing of the forests and building of extensive roadways. Thus, they are one of the few species that has benefitted by man's altering of the Adirondack environment. The woodchuck digs a complex system of burrows with multiple entrances. These burrows are often four feet deep, after which they level off to a bed and toilet chamber. The woodchuck has short, rounded ears which can be closed so that no dirt enters them during digging. They are homebodies, rarely travelling more than 150 feet from their burrows to feed. The burrows are later utilized by a variety of other animals.

Food: Favorite foods are grasses and other vegetation, some fruit, bark, twigs and cultivated crops. Woodchucks can wreak havoc with vegetable gardens. They rarely travel to get water; most of their liquid needs are satisfied by drinking dew.

Reproduction: Mating takes place early in the year, in March or April. After a gestation period of 30-33 days, a litter of 4-5 or more young is born.

Comments: The woodchuck shows its close relationship to other members of the squirrel family by occasionally climbing trees. It can also swim. In the fall, they build up layers of fat and in winter, they hibernate. At this time, their body temperature lowers to 37° and their heart rates slow to four or five beats per minute.

Woodchucks have four incisors which are used for gnawing plant matter. These teeth grow continuously, but grinding against one another keeps them both sharp and short. Should a woodchuck loose its lower incisors, the upper teeth will continue to grow, giving the animal a "saber-toothed" appearance. In extreme cases, these teeth continue to curl around until they kill the unfortunate creature by growing into the skull. Also known as the ground hog.

GRAY SQUIRREL
Sciurus carolinensis

Gray
Plate 12, No. 2, 3 & 4

Total length: 17-20 inches
Head and body: 8-10 inches
Tail: 8-10 inches
Weight: ³/₄ - 1¹/₄ pounds

Description: In summer the body is whitish gray intermixed with yellowish tints, especially on the upper back. The underparts are white. The face, top of the feet and shoulders display a more rusty coloration. The eyes are rimmed with white, and there is a white patch behind each ear. The long hairs of the tail have three color zones, brown to yellow-brown at the base, black in the middle, and whiter at the tips. In winter the coloration is a more even whitish gray, with less yellow mixed in. Melanistic black specimens, which do not have seasonal coloration changes, are not uncommon. White specimens have been recorded, but are rare.

Habitat: Gray squirrels prefer deciduous forests where oak and beech mast provides an important source of food. They build spherical nests of twigs and leaves high up in trees in which to raise their young.

Food: The squirrel's love of nuts is well known to even the most casual nature lovers. Grays store each nut individually in the ground, and are undoubtedly responsible for helping regenerate burned over and heavily cut hardwood areas. They also eat hickory nuts, walnuts, buds, corn, fungi, berries and fruit.

Reproduction: There are usually two breeding seasons, one mid to late winter and another midsummer. The gestation period is 42-45 days. Two litters of 2-3 (or more) young are born a year, the first March to April and the second July to August.

Comments: The gray, the largest of the Adirondack tree squirrels, is easily identified by its generally slate gray coloring and long bushy tail. The often-mentioned black squirrel is just a melanistic gray squirrel.

RED SQUIRREL
Tamiasciurus hudsonicus

Reddish Brown
Plate 13, No. 1 & 2

Total length: 11-13 inches
Head and body: 7-8 inches
Tail: 4-5 ½ inches
Weight: 5-8 ounces

Description: The red squirrel is unique in having not only seasonal color phases, but also stripes that appear or disappear with each color phase. In summer the upper body is reddish brown, gradually fading to a redder color on the legs and feet. There is a thin black stripe separating the colors of the upper body from the underside, which is white. The crown and ears match the color of the back, the sides of the face are paler and redder. The eyes are rimmed in white, and the lips and throat are white. The long hairs of the tail have three color zones, reddish brown at the base, black and then yellow near the tips, with the outer two color zones being larger and more obvious near the tip of the tail. In winter a broad stripe of bright chestnut red runs down the back, and the lower dark stripes fade away. The ears develop little tufts of chestnut hairs at the tips, and the underside may become grayer.

Habitat: Red squirrels are most at home in mixed and coniferous forests. They build spherical nests made up of leaves and twigs in the upper portions of favorite trees.

Food: Favorite foods include seeds of pine and other softwoods, mushrooms, berries, and bird eggs. During spring sap run, they will chew on maple buds, relishing the sweet taste.

Reproduction: They have two major breeding seasons, one February to March and another June to July. The gestation period is about 38 days. A litter of 4-5 or more young is born in April or May, another in August or September.

Comments: Red squirrels are determined gnawers who have been known to chew through thick rubber, plastic and even one-half inch plywood. When confronted, they will often stand their ground giving off challenging loud "clucks," even when their opponents are housecats. They are feisty little creatures who are an important link in the food chain, providing food for the hawk, marten, fisher, and other larger predators.

EASTERN/COMMON CHIPMUNK
Tamias striatus

Yellowish to Chestnut
Plate 13, No. 3

Total length: 8-10 inches
Head and body: 5-6½ inches
Tail: 2¾ - 3½ inches
Weight: 2-4 ounces

Description: The beautifully colored body is prominently marked by five almost black stripes. A pair of stripes extend along each side from the shoulder to the hip, the area between these stripes being pale yellow or buff. The entire area above these stripes, including the back, is a grizzled gray, bisected by the fifth black stripe, which runs from the crown to the tail. Below these stripes the sides of the body range from chestnut to yellowish red, with a sprinkling of darker hairs on the upper portions of each leg. The chin, throat and underparts are white. The head is similarly divided by colors. The crown shares the grizzled gray of the back, the eye is bordered above and below by two short pale buffy stripes, the area between these stripes and the cheeks is chestnut color. The upper surface of the tail is the salt-and-pepper of the back, the undersurface is paler and tinged with fawn.

Habitat: Chipmunks are found throughout the hardwood forests of the Adirondacks. Favorite hideouts for chipmunks are in firewood piles, under homes, and beneath fallen logs. In these areas, they inhabit a system of burrows, often with several entrances. They are marked by two-inch openings in the ground, are often two yards long and one yard deep. They have different areas for feeding, emitting waste and sleeping. The chipmunk is not active in winter, and is in a state of near hibernation in its burrow.

Food: In spring, the chipmunk will emerge from its burrow in search of foods such as nuts, seeds, and small invertebrates. As the seasons progress, wild fruits and fungi are added to its diet.

Reproduction: Chipmunks have two major breeding seasons, March to April and June to July. After a gestation period of about 31 days, a litter of 4-5 or more young are born.

Comments: They are an important food source for a number of predators including hawks, martens, weasels and foxes.

FLYING SQUIRRELS

Flying squirrels are the least known and least seen of the Adirondack squirrels. Attractive looking and secretive, they are strictly nocturnal creatures, and so are more often identified by the sound they emit rather than by actually sightings. This sound is a combination of insect-like chirps and mouse-like squeaks. Flying squirrels don't fly, but glide through the air in a graceful 45° descent with their fur-covered membrane stretched out and have been known to glide over 90 feet. The most unmistakable signs they leave are square imprints with accompanying tail marks in the snow where they land.

Habitat: Flying squirrels, like gray squirrels, prefer mixed or hardwood forests with ample food supplies. They build nests of twigs in tree cavities and old woodpecker holes. Like red squirrels, southern flying squirrels sometimes nest in attics.

Food: Favorite foods are acorns and beechnuts. They also feed on other seeds, fruit, fungi and some invertebrates.

Reproduction: Flying squirrels mate between February and April, with the southern species usually mating a few weeks before their northern relatives. Their gestation period runs from 38-40 days. A litter of 3-5 or more young is born in late spring or early summer. A second mating often takes place in midsummer, producing a second litter in late summer.

SOUTHERN FLYING SQUIRREL
Glaucomys volans

Grayish Brown
Plate 14, No. 1 & 2

Total length: 8½-11 inches
Head and body: 5-6 inches
Tail: 4-5 inches
Weight: 1¾-3 ounces

Description: Head, upper body and upper surface of the gliding membrane are grayish brown. The outer margin of the membrane is very dark blackish brown. The fur on the underside is pure white. The eyes are rimmed in black. The upper surface of the tail matches the grayish brown of the body, the undersurface is grayish to cream white. In winter the colors appear somewhat duller.

Comments: Formerly known as *Sciuropterus volans*.

NORTHERN FLYING SQUIRREL   Cinnamon Brown
Glaucomys sabrinus   Plate 13, No. 4

Total length: 10-12 inches
Head and body: 5½ - 6½ inches
Tail: 4½ - 5½ inches
Weight: 2-4½ ounces

Description: The head, upper body and upper surface of the gliding membrane are cinnamon brown to fawn brown. The outer margin of the gliding membrane is very dark blackish brown. The fur on the underside is bicolored, appears white but has a leaden gray base. The eyes are rimmed in black. The upper surface of the tail matches the brown color of the body, the undersurface is a lighter tan-brown. In winter the body is sooty brown, and the underparts become tinged with yellow.

Comments: Formerly known as *Sciuropterus sabrinus*.

Photo Section

Red Fox
Vulpes vulpes

Due to the rarity of this species, it was impossible to obtain a photo of a live specimen.

Page 18

2. Pygmy Shrew
Microsorex hoyi

Page 18

4. Smoky Shrew
Sorex fumeus

Page 17

1. Short-Tailed Shrew
Blarina brevicauda

Page 18

3. Masked Shrew
Sorex cinereus

PLATE 2

63

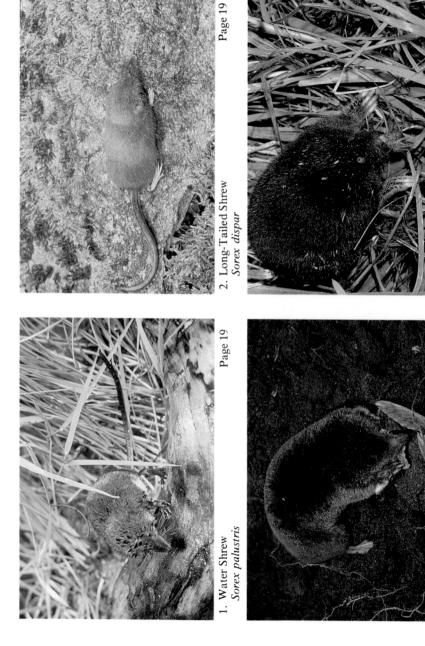

Page 19

2. Long-Tailed Shrew
Sorex dispar

Page 21

4. Star-Nosed Mole
Condylura cristata

Page 19

1. Water Shrew
Sorex palustris

Page 21

3. Hairy-Tailed Mole
Parascalops breweri

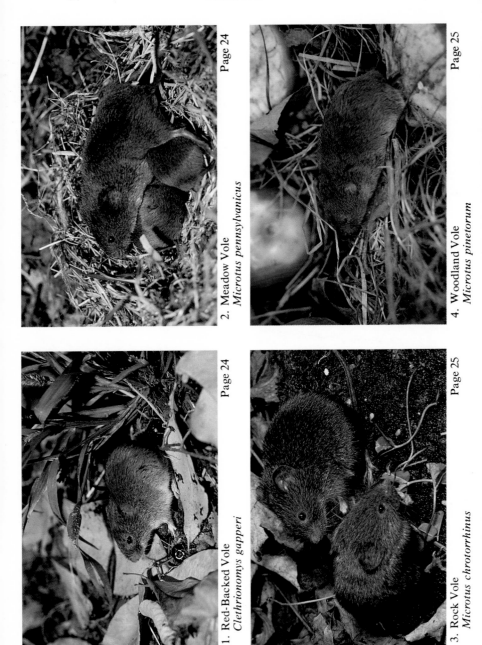

Page 24

2. Meadow Vole
Microtus pennsylvanicus

Page 25

4. Woodland Vole
Microtus pinetorum

Page 24

1. Red-Backed Vole
Clethrionomys gapperi

Page 25

3. Rock Vole
Microtus chrotorrhinus

PLATE 4 65

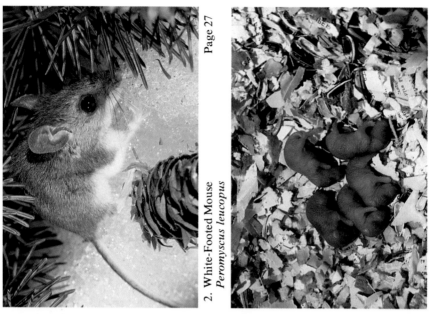

Page 27

2. White-Footed Mouse
Peromyscus leucopus

Page 27

4. Baby White-Footed Mouse
Peromyscus leucopus

Page 25

1. Southern Bog Lemming
Synaptomys cooperi

Page 27

3. Deer Mouse
Peromyscus maniculatus

1. Woodland Jumping Mouse
Napaeozapus insignis
Page 29

2. Meadow Jumping Mouse
Zapus hudsonius
Page 29

3. House Mouse
Mus musculus
Page 31

4. Norway Rat
Rattus norvegicus
Page 32

PLATE 6

67

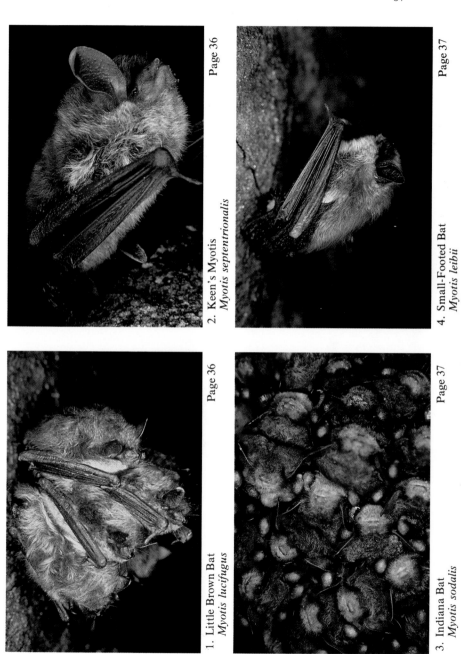

Page 36

2. Keen's Myotis
Myotis septentrionalis

Page 37

4. Small-Footed Bat
Myotis leibii

Page 36

1. Little Brown Bat
Myotis lucifugus

Page 37

3. Indiana Bat
Myotis sodalis

Page 38

2. Eastern Pipistrelle
Pipistrellus subflavus

Page 39

4. Red Bat
Lasiurus borealis

Page 38

1. Silver-Haired Bat
Lasionycteris noctivagans

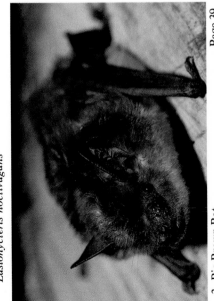

Page 39

3. Big Brown Bat
Eptesicus fuscus

PLATE 8

69

2. Typical Bat Cave

Page 40

1. Hoary Bat
Lasiurus cinereus

4. Beaver Dam

Page 42

3. Beaver
Castor canadensis

Page 44

2. Young Opossum
Didelphis virginiana

Page 46

4. Young Muskrat
Ondatra zibethicus

Page 44

1. Opossum
Didelphis virginiana

Page 46

3. Muskrat
Ondatra zibethicus

PLATE 10   71

Page 49

2. Young Snowshoe Rabbit
Lepus americanus

Page 51

4. Baby Eastern Cottontail
Sylvilagus floridanus

Page 49

1. Snowshoe Rabbit, winter coloration
Lepus americanus

Page 50

3. European Hare
Lepus europaeus

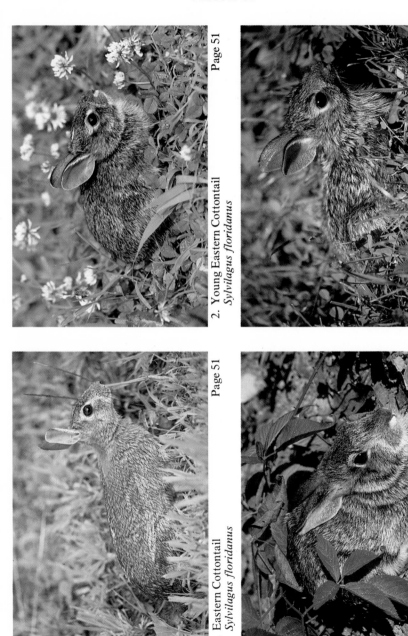

Page 51

2. Young Eastern Cottontail
Sylvilagus floridanus

Page 52

4. Young New England Cottontail
Sylvilagus transitionalis

Page 51

1. Eastern Cottontail
Sylvilagus floridanus

Page 52

3. New England Cottontail
Sylvilagus transitionalis

PLATE 12   73

Page 56

2. Gray Squirrel, white specimen
Sciurus carolinensis

Page 56

4. Young Gray Squirrel
Sciurus carolinensis

Page 54

1. Woodchuck
Marmota monax

Page 56

3. Gray Squirrel
Sciurus carolinensis

Page 57

2. Red Squirrel, winter coloration
Tamiasciurus hudsonicus

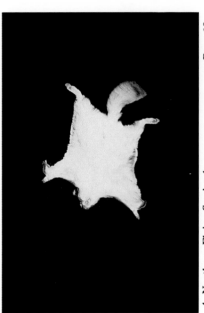

Page 60

4. Northern Flying Squirrel
Glaucomys sabrinus

Page 57

1. Red Squirrel, summer coloration
Tamiasciurus hudsonicus

Page 58

3. Eastern/Common Chipmunk
Tamias striatus

PLATE 14   75

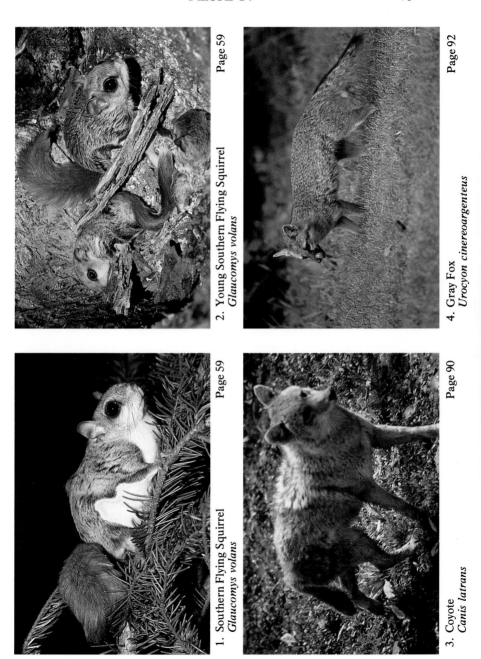

1. Southern Flying Squirrel
Glaucomys volans   Page 59

2. Young Southern Flying Squirrel
Glaucomys volans   Page 59

3. Coyote
Canis latrans   Page 90

4. Gray Fox
Urocyon cinereoargenteus   Page 92

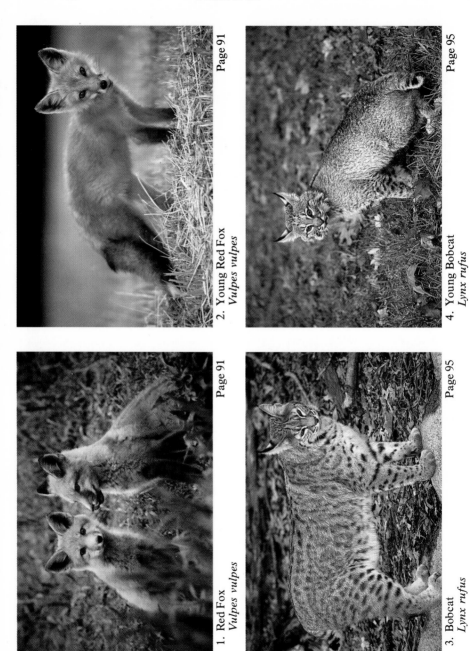

Page 91

2. Young Red Fox
Vulpes vulpes

Page 95

4. Young Bobcat
Lynx rufus

Page 91

1. Red Fox
Vulpes vulpes

Page 95

3. Bobcat
Lynx rufus

PLATE 16

77

Page 98

2. Porcupine
Erethizon dorsatum

Page 100

4. Raccoon, melanistic coloration
Procyon lotor

Page 96

1. Lynx
Lynx canadensis

Page 100

3. Raccoon
Procyon lotor

Page 105

2. Young Striped Skunk
Mephitis mephitis

Page 106

4. Otter
Lutra canadensis

Page 105

1. Striped Skunk
Mephitis mephitis

Page 106

3. Otter
Lutra canadensis

PLATE 18   79

1. Fisher, summer coloration
Martes pennanti
Page 107

2. Fisher, winter coloration
Martes pennanti
Page 107

3. Young Fisher
Martes pennanti
Page 107

4. Marten
Martes americana
Page 108

2. Long-Tailed Weasel
Mustela frenata

Page 111

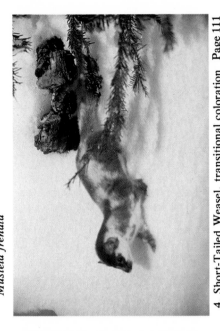

4. Short-Tailed Weasel, transitional coloration   Page 111
Mustela erminea

Page 110

1. Mink
Mustela vision

3. Short-Tailed Weasel, summer coloration   Page 111
Mustela erminea

PLATE 20   81

Page 115

2. Bull Moose, fall
   Alces alces

Page 115

3. Cow Moose, with calf
   Alces alces

Page 115

1. Bull Moose, summer
   Alces alces

Page 116

1. Whitetail Deer
Odocoileus virginianus

PLATE 22

83

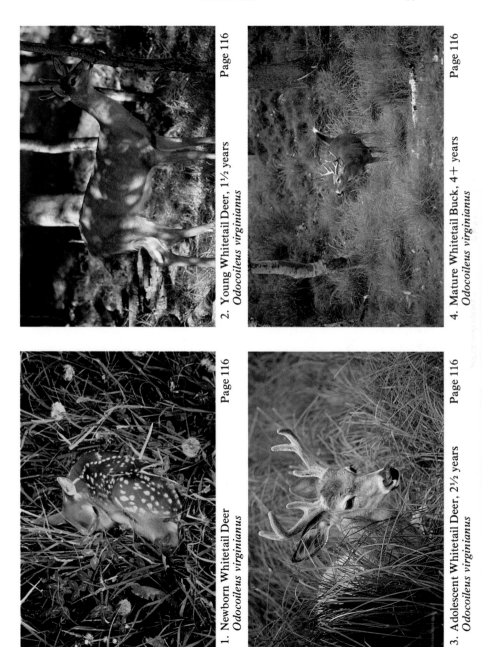

2. Young Whitetail Deer, 1½ years
Odocoileus virginianus
Page 116

4. Mature Whitetail Buck, 4+ years
Odocoileus virginianus
Page 116

1. Newborn Whitetail Deer
Odocoileus virginianus
Page 116

3. Adolescent Whitetail Deer, 2½ years
Odocoileus virginianus
Page 116

Page 116

2. Whitetail Buck in deer yard
Odocoileus virginianus

Page 116

4. Whitetail Deer, winter coloration
Odocoileus virginianus

Page 116

1. Whitetail Doe
Odocoileus virginianus

Page 116

3. Whitetail Deer, summer coloration
Odocoileus virginianus

PLATE 24   85

1. Black Bear   Page 119
   Ursus americanus

2. Young Black Bear   Page 119
   Ursus americanus

1. Man — William Chapman in summer attire, with beaver tree.   Page 121
    Homo sapiens

PLATE 26 87

Page 124

2. Badger
Taxidea taxus

Page 126

4. Young Timber Wolf
Canis lupus

Page 124

1. Wolverine
Gulo luscus

Page 126

3. Gray Timber Wolf
Canis lupus

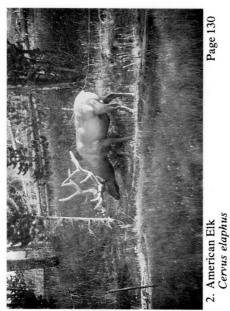

Page 128

Page 130

1. Mountain Lion
Felis concolor

2. American Elk
Cervus elaphus

Page 131

Page 132

3. Harbor Seal
Phoca vitulina

4. Wild Boar
Sus scrofa

CANINES
Canidae family

Members of this family are dog-like in outline, with long legs and bushy tails. The heads have elongated, pointed muzzles and upright triangular ears. The feet have dull, non-retractile claws.

There are currently three wild species of the canine family inhabiting the Adirondacks: the coyote, the gray fox and the red fox. The gray wolf, also known as the timber wolf, had an established breeding population here. In 1871 the state began paying bounties for wolf kills, and by the turn of the century the species had been decimated past the point of no return. Occasional stragglers were later encountered, but their breeding base had been destroyed. The last documented sighting of a wolf in the Adirondacks that I am aware of occurred in the 1960's, but this animal almost certainly originated outside the Park, and probably was not part of a vestige resident population. Current stories of wolf sightings are likely based on large coyotes, for the two often have similar coloration patterns.

KEY TO THE CANINES

I. Tail less than ½ combined head and body length, moderately bushy. Total length 3-4 feet long, brownish. Coyote, *Canis latrans*. Page 90.

II. Tail more than ½ combined head and body length, very bushy. Total length about 3 feet long.

   A. Body rusty red, tail white-tipped. Red Fox, *Vulpes vulpes*. Page 91.

   B. Body grizzled gray, tail with a distinct black stripe. Gray Fox, *Urocyon cinereoargenteus*. Page 92.

COYOTE   Light Brown
Canis latrans   Plate 14, No. 3

Total length: 38-48 inches
Head and body: 25-32 inches
Tail: 13-15 inches
Height at shoulder: 22-24 inches
Weight: 20-35 pounds

Description: The general body color is light brown to reddish brown, heavily grizzled with an intermixture of both blacker and paler hairs. The black hairs often form a dark ridge along the back. The outer surface of the legs, back of the ears and especially the crown is brown-tinged. The throat, chest and undersurface are pale buff to white. The tail is grayish brown with a dark stripe above, paler beneath, and black-tipped. Individual specimens vary considerably in the degree of brown or gray predominating their coloration. The skins of coyote and of the gray wolf are almost impossible to differentiate.

Habitat: A relative newcomer to the Adirondacks, the coyotes arrived in New York State in the 1920s from southern Ontario, and were firmly established by the 1950s. Today they can be found in such diverse habitats as the High Peaks wilderness region, the Champlain Valley and the outskirts of cities such as Plattsburgh. They may den up in hollow logs, under fallen timber or underground burrows.

Food: They are opportunistic feeders and will eat mice, rabbits, apples, berries, grasses, carrion, dump refuse, deer, and domestic animals.

Reproduction: The coyote mates in late winter. After a gestation period of about 60 days, a litter of approximately 6 pups is born in April or May.

Comments: Differentiating coyote from dog tracks can be difficult, but coyote tracks are generally in a straight line with one print right behind the other. Dog tracks are often side by side and rambling. Another coyote trademark is its distinctive howl, high pitched and plaintive. The coyote is sometimes called the bushwolf, perhaps in a romantic attempt to keep alive the memory of the now missing gray wolf. Dogs, wolves and coyotes are all closely related, and capable of interbreeding. Coydogs, a cross between coyotes and dogs, were reported in New York soon after the first coyote appeared here. Contrary to popular belief, documented recordings of coydogs have become practically nonexistant since the coyote populations dramatically increased in the late 1950s.

Scientific research is just beginning to shed new light on this wily predator. Initial findings from Canada indicate that the coyote, on its journey eastward through southern Canada during the early part of this century, interbred with timber wolves. This is probably the reason for the eastern coyotes' increased size, considerably larger than western coyote. Although the timber wolf may be extirpated from the Adirondacks, the lonely cry of its bushwolf cousin now echoes throughout the mountains.

RED FOX   Rusty Red
Vulpes vulpes   Plate 15, No. 1 & 2

Total length: 35-40 inches
Head and body: 22-24 inches
Tail: 13-16 inches
Height at shoulder: about 15 inches
Weight: 7-11 pounds

Description: The body and head are rusty red, brightest on the shoulders. The red of the hindquarters, outer surface of the legs and the face is intermixed with a light sprinkling of grayish hairs. The front of the ears, throat, undersurface and insides of the legs are white. The feet, front of the legs and tips of the back ear surface are dark brown or black. The tail is rusty red, with darker hairs on the upper surface and white-tipped. Many color phases exist, from very pale yellowish red to solid black.

Habitat: Although found in a variety of habitats in northern New York, red fox prefer open land like old pastures, farm fields and beaver meadows. Red fox are very adaptable, and in winters of extreme cold and snow, they will congregate near deer yards in search of dead deer. These stealthy predators are becoming more frequently seen near Adirondack towns. One theory has it that they are being driven from more remote areas by increasing coyote populations. Their dens are typically found in underground burrows, or sometimes hollow logs.

Food: The red fox's distinctive erect ears and pointed snout are appropriate physical characteristics for an animal that relies heavily on hearing and smell when hunting. When a red fox hunts for field mice, it will first smell the area for mouse scent, then listen for movement. If a mouse is nearby, the fox will execute a flying leap and pounce upon it. Other favorite foods are rabbits, squirrels, chipmunks, woodchucks, grouse and carrion. Red fox are fond of both fresh and older fermenting apples in the fall and early winter. They also feast on released pheasants when they are available.

Reproduction: Mating takes place in mid to late winter. Following a gestation period of 51-53 days, a litter averaging 6 pups is born in March or April.

Comments: It is hard to confuse the red fox with any other animal in the Adirondacks, for it is the only animal that appears so predominantly red. Formerly known as *Vulpes fulvus* and *Vulpes fulva*.

GRAY FOX   Speckled Gray
Urocyon cinereoargenteus   Plate 14, No. 4

Total length: 35-40 inches
Head and body: 23-26 inches
Tail: 12-15 inches
Height at shoulder: about 14 inches
Weight: 7-11 pounds

Description: Back and most of the body gray, strongly grizzled by black and white bands on the hair. Most of the face is a flecked gray like the body. The front of the ears are edged in white, the rear surface is chestnut red with dark gray tips. The sides of the neck and the breast form an unbroken band of bright chestnut red. The throat and undersurface of the body are white, with an indistinct band of red on the sides separating the white areas from the gray. The outer surfaces of the legs are a mixture of gray and red, the inner surfaces pale reddish brown. The upper surface of the tail is gray with a prominent black stripe running to the tip, pale chestnut red beneath.

Habitat: The Adirondacks are close to the northern limit of the gray fox's range. Probably nowhere in the Adirondacks is the gray fox plentiful. It is most common in the southern Adirondacks, and the Champlain and St. Lawrence Valleys. Gray foxes live in hardwood forests, where they den in sheltered areas such as hollow logs or under fallen trees.

Food: Favorite foods include birds, especially ruffed grouse, bird eggs, rabbits, insects, mice and berries.

Reproduction: The mating season runs from mid winter into spring. Following a gestation period of 51-55 days a litter of 3-6 pups will be born, usually in March or April.

Comments: Where gray and red foxes inhabit the same area, one way to tell the difference is to focus on the animal's tracks. Sooner or later gray fox tracks will end near a leaning tree since the gray fox, unlike the red, has the ability to climb trees. They will also leap into the lower branches of trees where they can be found taking a midday nap a good eight feet above the ground. Gray foxes prefer hardwood forests where they can utilize their tree climbing ability to escape from their enemies, usually domestic dogs or man.

FELINES
Felidae family

Life has not been easy for the three members of the cat family that naturally occurred within the Adirondacks. By the turn of the last century both the mountain lion and the lynx had all but vanished; the mountain lion a victim of over hunting and the lynx from loss of habitat due to excessive logging. The more adaptable bobcat actually extended its range within the park as the forests were cleared, but its inability to contend with severe mountain winters has limited its population to lower elevations.

KEY TO THE FELINES

I. Body medium, 2-3 feet long. Tail short, only 4-6 inches.
   A. Feet not large, leaving tracks about 2 inches long by 2 inches wide. Body often conspicuously spotted. Ear tips slightly tufted or not tufted at all. Tip of tail black on upper surface only. Bobcat, *Lynx rufus*. Page 95.
   B. Legs disproportionately long, feet very large, leaving tracks about 3½ inches long and wide. Body not conspicuously spotted. Ear tips distinctly tufted. Tip of tail black all around. Lynx, *Lynx canadensis*. Page 96.

BOBCAT
Tan Brown
Lynx rufus
Plate 15, No. 3 & 4

Head and body: 25-35 inches
Tail: 4-6 inches
Height at shoulder: 12-15 inches
Weight: 15-35 pounds

Description: The body is tan brown, darker on the head and back, and lightening to dull white below the chin, throat and belly. The body and sides of legs usually have dark brown to black spots. The face is handsomely marked with narrow dark bars. The back of the ears is black, surrounding a large white patch, and the tips are slightly tufted. The upper surface of the tail has several dark horizontal stripes and a black tip, the underside is pale and unmarked. In summer the fur/hair is very short, and reddish tinged. In winter the coat is grayer, lighter in color and thicker.

Habitat: Bobcats are widely dispersed throughout the Adirondacks, with southern areas containing the highest numbers. In the more remote sections where there is heavy winter snowfall, they are not found above 2,500 feet elevation because their relatively small paws provide little buoyancy in the deep snow. Bobcats build dens of dried grass in caves or in hollow trees.

Food: Because they evolved in more southern climes where competition among other predators was greater, bobcats are generalized carnivores which eat rabbits, mice, squirrels, chipmunks, ruffed grouse, and deer. They will also chew on grasses and leaves.

Reproduction: Mating takes place early in the year, from late February through March. Following a gestation period of 55 to 62 days, one to four (usually two) kittens are born in late April or May.

Comments: Although about twice the size of large domestic cats, they appear even larger because their long legs and short tails accentuate their body size. The screeching cry of a bobcat is like that of any city alley cat but magnified many times.

Though originally a southern species, the presence of bobcats along with boreal species like lynx and moose help make the Adirondacks one of the most unique wilderness areas in the east. Formerly listed as *Felis rufus*.

LYNX   Brownish Gray
Lynx canadensis   Plate 16, No. 1

Head and body: 25-35 inches
Tail: 4-6 inches
Height at shoulder: 14-16 inches
Weight: 15-35 pounds

Description: In summer the upper body is grayish with brown tints, darkest on the head and along the back. The color fades to dull white on the chin, throat and belly. There may be a few darker spots on the inner surfaces of the limbs. The facial ruff is usually marked with darker bars. Back of ears black surrounding a large white patch. Ear tips are distinctly tufted. The upper surface of the tail is the color of the back, tipped with black all around. In winter the fur is longer, thicker and a paler gray. The body of the young is marked by a pattern of rosettes and bars not unlike those of the ocelot, but this fades away early in life.

Habitat: Lynx can be found inhabiting older forests in the High Peaks area. They are well adapted to life at the higher elevations. Their large round feet act as natural snowshoes, and their thick fur provides protection against the winter cold. They den in hollow trees or similarly sheltered places.

Food: The lynx evolved in the far north where there were less predators to compete with, so it became a specialized hunter of snowshoe rabbits, which make up the largest percentage of their diet. Fortunately for the lynx, the Adirondack snowshoe population is relatively stable and a dependable food source. This is in contrast to the situation found in Canada, where widely fluctuating snowshoe population cycles put it in danger of starvation during years of snowshoe scarcity. During such years, they travel great distances in search of food.

Reproduction: The mating season for lynx takes place in March. Following a gestation period of about 60 days, a litter of one to four (usually two) kittens is born in May.

Comments: Lynx can be confused with bobcats where both share the same range and this potential overlap exists in sections of the Adirondacks. They have longer legs than bobcats and thicker fur, which make the lynx appear larger than the bobcat, even though their weights are comparable. Like most cats, they leave little sign. Except for tracks found in the snow at higher elevations or a distinctive scream tapering off to a long wail, few people would know the solitary lynx is in the area.

The lynx originally inhabited the Adirondack mountains, but due to habitat loss by extensive logging this cat had vanished from the area by the end of the 19th century. Occasionally lynx have been seen in New York during this century, but there was no resident breeding population. In the late 1980s an attempt was begun by the Adirondack Wildlife Program of the SUNY College of Environmental Science and Forestry in cooperation with the New York State Department of Environmental Conservation to release live trapped lynx from the Yukon into the High Peaks region. This area was selected partially because of a plentiful snowshoe hare population. At the time of this writing in 1990, as a result of this program over 30 lynx again roam the Adirondacks, and plans are in place for future releases. Each of these animals was fitted with a radio tracking collar. Although these collars are usually out of sight beneath their thick fur, if you are fortunate enough to spot one of these animals you may also see six or seven inches of radio antenna! At this point it appears that the automobile is one of the most potent dangers they face. If you are going to be motoring in the high peaks area, please use all possible caution to avoid the loss of any more of these beautiful cats. It is hoped that with the assistance of the restocking effort, the lynx will once again occupy its rightful place in northern New York. Formerly known as *Felis lynx*.

PORCUPINE
Erithizontidae family

Short, plump and appearing larger than it really is (particularly when upset with quills erect), the porcupine seems fearless as it plods through Adirondack campsites in search of salt. In fact, porcupines seem to be able to sense salt, whether it be from a sweat covered ax handle or an old salt lick. Rural homes where rock salt is used in winter become favorite spring haunts for porcupines.

PORCUPINE	Frosted Black
Erethizon dorsatum	Plate 16, No. 2

Total length: 25-36 inches
Head and body: 20-28 inches
Tail: 6-10 inches
Weight: 15-25 pounds

Description: Porcupines have medium-size, thick-set bodies with short limbs. They have short-faced, rounded heads with small ears. The feet are armed with prominent hooked claws, used for climbing. The tail is short and thick. The body is covered with remarkably long hair, up to six inches in length. The porcupine's best known feature is the 2-4 inch long quills, modified hairs used for defense and found covering most of the body save the undersurfaces.

The body is brown to dark brown to nearly black on all surfaces, with slight lightening in color on the undersurface and the sides of the tail. The body has a very noticeable grizzled or hoary appearance due to the intermixing of hairs and quills. The black body hairs, especially on the shoulders, are white tipped, and the quills are dirty white with dark tips.

Habitat: Porcupines prefer to inhabit mixed forests with a good supply of both coniferous and broad-leaved trees. They den in sheltered areas such as small caves or hollow logs.

Food: When available, they consume fruit, seeds, grasses and some leaves. In winter, they eat the bark of various evergreens such as hemlock and spruce, and also that of birch, aspen and maple. A sure sign that porcupines are in the area is the presence of gnawed and girdled trees (unlike the beaver, porcupines do not gnaw in a symetrical pattern).

Reproduction: The porcupine's unusually vocal mating season takes place in November or December. The gestation period is surprisingly long, about 6½ months. Usually a single young is born in May or June.

Comments: With the increase in the Adirondack fisher population in the past 20 years, porcupine numbers have dropped considerably, as has the forest damage they cause. The fisher is one of the few predators that knows how to kill a porcupine effectively. Automobiles also take their toll of porcupines in northern New York.

RACCOON
Procyonidae family

With its ringed tail and masked face, the raccoon looks unlike any other animal inhabiting the Adirondacks. Coons have dainty "hands" that seem almost too small to support their chubby bodies. These "hands" are perfect for capturing fresh water mussels, frogs and snakes in water. Because raccoons get lots of food from aquatic sources, people have come to believe that they wash their dinner before eating it, but there is no scientific evidence to support this.

RACCOON   Yellowish Brown
Procyon lotor   Plate 16, No. 3 & 4

Total length: 25-36 inches
Head and body: 17-25 inches
Tail: 8-11 inches
Weight: 10-25 pounds

Description: The raccoon has a stout body, almost bear-like in outline, and is covered with long coarse hair. Its head is broad, with a pointed muzzle and triangular, erect ears. All feet have five fully developed toes with fixed, non-retractile claws. The tail is thick and bushy, about ½ the combined head and body length.

The body is yellowish gray to brownish gray. The longer hairs are black-tipped, giving the coat a speckled salt-and-pepper appearance. The underparts are a paler gray. The face is whitish, with a narrow black stripe running from the nose up between the eyes to the forehead. Each eye is surrounded by a large black patch, giving the raccoon its famous "masked" appearance. The ears are white-tipped. The tail is yellowish brown with about five black bands that do not meet on the underside, and black-tipped.

Habitat: The raccoon seems at home in all Adirondack habitats save the higher elevations. They prefer to live near water, and frequently choose to live in the immediate vicinity of man. They often den in hollow trees.

Food: They are omnivorous and will eat apples, berries, grapes and beechnuts, as well as mice and carrion. In agricultural sections of the mountains, it is almost impossible for farmers and gardeners to keep raccoons out of their corn. Raccoons are also extremely fond of aquatic foods such as fresh water mussels and clams.

Reproduction: The mating season takes place from February into March. Following a gestation period of 63 days, a litter of 3 to 6 young is born from April to May.

Comments: Signs of raccoons in the neighborhood are the easily identified tracks in the soft mud of a stream bank, broken clam shells, and overturned garbage cans in the more settled areas. The Adirondacks are close to the northern limit of this amusing omnivore.

WEASEL FAMILY
Mustelidae family

Members of the weasel family (skunk, badger and wolverine excepted) usually have long slender bodies. They have short legs, and five toes with nonretractile claws on each foot. Heads may vary from triangular to rounded, usually with small ears. The form of the tail is highly variable and often a key identification feature.

Few animal families are as diverse as this family. While most of its members are known for their fierce temperments, the semi-aquatic otter and the comical skunk are considered as fun loving, even gentle creatures. Some members are terrestrial, some arboreal (living in trees), and some semi-aquatic. Most members of the weasel family have solid coloration on their upper bodies, yet the closely related skunk and wolverine wear distinctive stripes. One feature that most family members have in common is that the females tend to be much smaller than the males. Feeding habits are also similar. Family members will locate an area with good cover and abundant prey. They will stay in one area until they have depleted much of their food source, and then move on in search of their next temporary home.

One of the more remarkable characteristics of the *Mustelidae* family is the length and variability of the gestation period. This occurs because the *Mustelidae* are among those animals whose young do not begin development immediately after mating. A female wolverine, for example, may mate in June, but the young inside her will not develop until the winter season. This explains why some members of this family have been recorded as not giving birth for more than a full year after mating.

The "true" weasels are easily differentiated from other members of this family by their pure white winter camouflage. A third true weasel *Mustela nivalis* (was *Putorious rixosa* and *M. rixosa*) is a resident of the southern border of New York State. In summer it is dark reddish brown above and pure white below, but it differs in coloration from other weasels by not having a black tip on its tail. It is a small weasel, about six inches long, of which only one inch is tail. This little fighter usually weighs in at under two ounces. This least weasel, as it is commonly called, is frequently described as the smallest carnivore in North America. This description is largely a matter of semantics, for although it is the smallest member of the order *Carnivora*, it is still much larger than a pygmy shrew (*Microsorex hoyi*), a meat-eating (carnivorous) member of the order *Insectivora*. Some older books have stated that the least weasel is found throughout the Adirondacks, but it is our opinion that this is an error, possibly based on misidentifications.

The fourth weasel, the New York or black-tailed weasel (*Putorius noveboracensis*) is listed as an Adirondack resident in most older natural history books. The New York weasel was described as having a dark brown body, approximately 15 inches long, of which about ⅓ was a black-tipped tail. The disappearance of this weasel from current natural history books is not to be taken as an indication that it has passed into extinction. Instead, it has merely been reclassified as only a variety of the far-from-extinct long-tailed weasel.

KEY TO THE WEASEL FAMILY

 I. Body thick-set, stocky. Tail very bushy, about ⅓ total length. Body black with conspicuous V-shaped white striping. Striped Skunk, *Mephitis mephitis*. Page 105.

 II. Body long and tapering. Tail also long and tapering, not bushy, about ⅓ total length. Semi-aquatic, with webbed feet. 36-48 inches long. Otter, *Lutra canadensis*. Page 106.

 III. Body long and slender, tail bushy. Body color not turning white in winter.

    A. Large, 36-40 inches long. Body grayish brown to brownish black. Tail about 40% total length. Arboreal (tree dwelling). Fisher, *Martes pennanti*. Page 107.

    B. 20-25 inches long. Body yellow-brown to orange-brown. Tail about ⅓ total length. Arboreal. Marten, *Martes americana*. Page 108.

    C. 18-24 inches long. Body dark brown, almost black. Tail about ⅓ total length. Semi-aquatic, toes partially webbed. Mink, *Mustela vision*. Page 110.

 IV. Body long and slender; tail slightly bushy and black-tipped. Fur becoming white in winter.

    A. 12-18 inches long. Tail just over ⅓ total length. Feet brown in summer. Long-Tailed Weasel, *Mustela frenata*. Page 111.

    B. 8-12 inches long. Tail about ¼ total length. Feet white in summer. Short-Tailed Weasel, *Mustela erminea*. Page 111.

STRIPED SKUNK   Black and White
Mephitis mephitis   Plate 17, No. 1 & 2

Total length: 20-25 inches
Head and body: 13-16 inches
Tail: 7-10 inches
Weight: 7-10 pounds

Description: The body is thick-set and covered with very long hair. The head has a pointed snout and short ears. The tail is large and bushy. The overall color is black, with the following exceptions; a thin white blaze runs from the forehead down between the eyes almost reaching the nose and the body is marked with a prominent white V-shaped design. The apex of the "V" covers the shoulders just behind the head and sometimes includes the crown and ears. This divides into two side stripes, one running along each side back to the tail. The tail is usually marked with white, which may vary from a continuation of the stripes on the sides to a less distinct scattering of white hairs throughout. The size of the white body stripe varies considerably from almost lacking to being so large as to make the animal mostly white.

Habitat: Skunks are found throughout the Adirondacks, and are often found living close to human habitations. Usually they inhabit underground burrows.

Food: They are omnivorous, eating wild fruits and greens, insects and other invertebrates, small reptiles and amphibians, birds and their eggs, and small rodents. Skunks are not above raiding garbage cans or farmyards for food. Along lake shorelines, especially Lake Champlain, pieces of turtle eggs littered about the beaches are sure signs that they are in the vicinity.

Reproduction: Skunks usually mate in February or March. Following a gestation period of 60-70 days, they give birth to a litter of 4-6 or more young in late April or May.

Comments: Unlike the rest of the weasel family, they do not remain active all year long. During the coldest parts of the Adirondack winter they remain underground in a state of limited activity. Use caution in all dealings with skunks, for in addition to their well known, highly offensive spray, they have also been known to carry rabies.

OTTER
Seal Brown
Lutra canadensis
Plate 17, No. 3 & 4

Total length: 36-48 inches
Head and body: 25-30 inches
Tail: 12-17 inches
Weight: 10-20 pounds

Description: The otter has a long and slender body with short legs and webbed feet. The tail is very broad at the base, tapering to a point, roughly ⅓ the total length. The head is broad with a blunt nose and small ears. (With its rounded head and long drooping whiskers, an otter's head is almost reminiscent of an old walrus caricature.) Females are slightly smaller than males. Semi-aquatic.

The upper body, tail, legs and feet a uniform glossy seal-brown. The underparts range from pale brown to grayish brown. The lips, cheeks, chin and throat are grizzled with numerous gray hairs.

Habitat: The ideal habitat is an area with numerous ponds and small lakes interconnected by streams. Otter dens are highly variable in form, ranging from leafy nests under fallen timber to underground burrows. In winter, otters use a series of air holes around a pond to travel between water and the shore. Their winter trails can be easily spotted and look like someone dragged a six-inch pipe through the snow. Upon closer examination, one will see large parallel tracks on the borders of the trough.

Food: Favorite foods are fish, frogs, crayfish, fresh-water mussels and, reportedly, young muskrats and ducks.

Reproduction: The mating season for otters runs from late winter to early spring. After an extended gestation period a litter of 1-5 young are born in late winter to early spring the following year.

Comments: Because otters are water-based predators, they have almost no competition for food from other species. As a result, they often appear to spend an inordinate amount of time at play.

FISHER
Martes pennanti

Very Dark Brown
Plate 18, No. 1, 2 & 3

Total length: 36-40 inches
Head and body: 22-25 inches
Tail: 14-16 inches
Weight: 8-12 pounds

Description: Fishers' bodies are longer and stockier than that of most other weasel-like animals. Their legs are short. The head is short with a pointed muzzle and prominent ears. The tail is full and bushy.

Their color is variable, dark grayish brown to brownish black. The foreparts often intermixed with white hairs, the posterior end darker brown. The sides are lighter, the underparts range from brown to tan. The snout, back of the ears, throat, legs and tail darker, sometimes black. Young fishers are predominantly gray. They turn brown upon adulthood, and when old appear almost black all over. The adult female is significantly smaller than the male.

Habitat: Fishers prefer hardwood and mixed forests where some tree succession is occurring. They may den in any sheltered area, occasionally the abandoned nests of other species.

Food: Fishers eat snowshoe rabbits, squirrels, rodents, and also occasionally feed on invertebrates, fruits and seeds. They are also one of the few animals that routinely kill and eat porcupines.

Reproduction: The mating season runs from late winter to early spring. After an extended gestation period of as much as one year, a litter of 1 to 5 young is born in late winter to early spring of the following year.

Comments: Some panther sightings were found to be large fisher. Reports of black panthers, a rare color phase almost nonexistent even in areas where panther populations are known to exist, were probably based on sightings of large, dark colored fisher. Probably the most plentiful sign left by the fisher is its tracks. Because it lopes in snow, the tracks often appear in clumps three feet apart, where tracks of the wild canines and felines are in a straight line. Also known as the fishercat, blackcat, Pekan and Pennant marten. Formerly known as *Mustela pennanti*.

MARTEN
Martes americana

Yellowish Brown
Plate 18, No. 4

Total length: 20-25 inches
Head and body: 13-17 inches
Tail: 6½-8 inches
Weight: 1½-2½ pounds

Description: In size, weight and bushiness of the tail, the marten stands intermediate between the smaller weasels and the larger fisher. Body weasel-like, with short legs. Head somewhat triangular, ears high and pointed. Tail about ⅓ total length, and bushy.

Body dark yellowish brown to orange-brown, darkest along the back, somewhat lighter beneath. Face grayish brown. The front of the ears are edged in dirty white, much darker behind. There is a large patch of yellowish orange on the throat and chest and a smaller one between the hind legs. Feet, legs and the upper surface of the tail very dark brown, approaching black. The undersurface of the tail has an orangish tinge and is black-tipped. Individuals may vary from almost black to paler and yellower with no tinges of orange visible.

Habitat: During the early part of this century, Adirondack forests were decimated because of unregulated and uncontrolled cutting. As a result, marten numbers dwindled until the animal was almost extirpated from northern New York. They need older climax forests, both mixed and softwood, to go about their business of procuring food. Today the High Peaks region contains the best marten habitat, since most of the land is state owned and much of the forest is returning to the climax stage. They den in hollow trees and logs.

Food: Marten feed on such diverse foods as red and flying squirrels, rabbits, mice, birds and their eggs, occasionally invertebrates or fruits and seeds. In areas where they are plentiful, it is not unusual for martens to visit campsites looking for free handouts. One of their favorite treats is peanut butter, which has also been used as bait by researchers to live trap the animal.

Reproduction: They mate in midsummer, but the young are not born until the following year, usually in April. Most litters are made up of 2-4 young.

Comments: Both marten and fisher may be found in the same habitat, higher elevation climax forests, and the easiest way to differentiate between the two is by their size and color. Martens are housecat-sized animals with light brown fur and an easily seen yellowish breast patch, whereas the fisher is larger and has much darker fur. The marten is sometimes mistaken for a squirrel when it is observed travelling through the treetops.

In recent years, the marten population has increased and animals are being seen more frequently outside the central Adirondacks. It is a boreal species common north of New York State, and its presence in moderate numbers here is a reminder of our ties to the great north woods of Canada.

Also known as the American marten, pine marten and American sable.

MINK
Mustela vision

Dark Brown, Glossy
Plate 19, No. 1

Total length: 18-24 inches
Head and body: 12-16 inches
Tail: 6-8 inches
Weight: $1^{1}/_{2}$ - $2^{1}/_{4}$ pounds

Description: Mink have long and slender bodies (weasel-like, but larger, heavier, with a thicker, bushier tail). The neck is long, head broadly triangular with short ears. Legs are short, and toes partially webbed, five toes front and behind. The tail is about $^{1}/_{3}$ total length and bushy. Females are smaller than the males. Semi-aquatic.

The body is dark brown, almost black, with many long, glossy guard hairs; color is even darker on the back and the tail. Underparts are a slightly lighter brown. There is a spot of white on the chin, and sometimes several other irregular white spots scattered about the underside.

Habitat: Mink are invariably found near water. They are known to inhabit burrows, old muskrat dens or even hollow logs.

Food: Mink are primarily aquatic feeders, taking fish, frogs, turtles, crayfish and snails. They will also hunt birds and their eggs and small mammals on land. Mink are particularly fond of muskrat flesh and probably influence significant control over muskrat populations.

Reproduction: Mink mate early in the year, from March to early April. Following a variable gestation period which can range from 40-65 days, a litter of 2-6 young is born in April or May.

Comments: Mink rarely travel far from water. In winter, they travel under ice, moving from air hole to air hole. These are good places to look for mink tracks since the animals often climb out of these holes and search nearby woods for food. Formerly known as *Putorius vision*.

LONG-TAILED WEASEL
Mustela frenata

Summer: Brown
Winter: White
Plate 19, No. 2

Total length: 12-18 inches
Head and body: 8-12 inches
Tail: 4¼ - 6¼ inches
Weight: 4-9 ounces

Description: In summer the upper body, legs and feet are brown, somewhat darker on the crown and back, lightest on the legs. The underside and throat are light buffy yellow, sometimes with a slight orange tinge. The tail matches the color of the back on both surfaces, and is black-tipped for about one third of its length. In winter all parts of the body except for the black tip of the tail turn snow white.

Habitat: The long-tail prefers to live in open grassy areas where it can hunt for its favorite food, the field mouse. It dens in abandoned burrows or in openings along rock faces.

Food: They are expert mousers and can penetrate all but the smallest mouse dens. It is estimated that one long-tail weasel will kill over 1,300 mice in one year. In addition to mice, long-tailed weasels also consume rabbits, birds and their eggs, and insects.

Reproduction: Long-tailed weasels mate in midsummer, and give birth to a litter of 4-8 or more young the following April or early May.

SHORT-TAILED WEASEL, ERMINE
Mustela erminea

Summer: Brown
Winter: White
Plate 19, No. 3 & 4

Total length: 8-12 inches
Head and body: 6-9 inches
Tail: 2-3¼ inches
Weight: 2-4 ounces

Description: In summer the upper parts are dark brown. The underparts, the feet and the throat are white, often with a yellow tinge. Both surfaces of the tail match the color of the upper body, except the tip which is black. In winter all parts of the body except for the black tip of the tail turn snow white. There may be a yellowish tinge on the rump and underparts during the winter phase.

Habitat: Ermine are found in thick forest cover. Preferred denning locations are old woodchuck burrows, under stumps and crevices in rock piles.

Food: Ermine are excellent mousers and will also kill and eat grouse, rabbits, squirrels, lemmings, voles and insects. They also feed on bird's eggs.

Reproduction: They mate in early summer, but the young are not born until April or May of the following year! Ermine usually give birth to 4-8 or more young per litter.

Comments: Like most other members of this family, weasels or ermine lope rather than walk, and when observed from a distance, their quickness and stealth are impressive as they undulate from hole to hole on rock ledges looking for food. In winter, weasel tracks are readily visible, but can be confused with squirrel tracks. One difference is that squirrel tracks are paired, each foot parallel to the other, whereas with weasel tracks, the left foot is placed slightly ahead of the right. Also, squirrel tracks are usually in a straight line, often going from one tree to another, while weasel tracks appear more random, showing where the animal has moved in and out of swale grass, logs or rocks in search of food.

Section III

Large Mammals

Black Bear
Ursus americanus

DEER FAMILY
Cervidae family

Two physical features immediately set the deer family apart from all other mammals: their split hooves and their fascinating antlers. Their large size, natural beauty and gentle reputation make them among the most popular of wild animals. Despite this popularity, deer have not had an easy time of it in the Adirondacks. Of the three species orginally known to live within the park, two, the moose and the elk, were extirpated more than a century ago. There were attempts to restock the elk earlier in this century, but it is believed that illegal hunting doomed this effort. The moose was also extirpated, but is currently attempting to reintroduce itself. There is a growing consensus that man should release additional moose in the park to reinforce this small, naturally occurring population. It will be an indication of our own species' growing maturity if these moose introductions meet with greater success the those of the ill-fated elk.

KEY TO THE DEER FAMILY

I. Body very large, 8-9 feet long and $5^{1}/_{2}$ - $6^{1}/_{2}$ feet tall at the shoulder. Body color very dark, with a pronounced hump on the shoulders. Only the males have antlers. Antlers wide and palmated (hand-like) with many points. Moose, *Alces alces*. Page 115.

II. Body large, 5-6 feet long and about 3 feet tall at the shoulder. Body color reddish brown to grayish brown. Only the males have antlers. Antlers not palmated, one main beam bearing additional upswept points. Whitetail Deer, *Odocoileus virginianus*. Page 116.

MOOSE
Alces alces

Total length: 96-108 inches
Height at shoulder: 66-78 inches
Tail: 2½-4 inches
Weight: 1,000-1,400 pounds

Description: The body is dark brown to almost black over most of its surface, including the undersides. The head is paler, browner, with the nose and lower jaw much darker than the rest of the head. The insides of the ears are grayish. The inner surfaces of the legs, the area between the hind legs, and the entire leg from the knee down are grayish. The hooves are black. The young are a dull reddish brown for the first few months of life. Moose antlers are wide and strongly palmated. Measurements of moose antlers in New England reveal many specimens with a spread of 40 to 55 inches and 20 to 26 points. Should New York's moose herd become reestablished, it is expected that animals of this size will soon be roaming the Adirondacks.

Habitat: Generally, good moose habitat is found in the Tug Hill area and the western Adirondacks up to St. Lawrence and Franklin Counties. Wet areas like bogs and swamps provide excellent summer habitat and are important to moose survival. The moose with its powerful piston-like legs is not hampered by deep snow (up to 3½ feet), so it is not forced to "yard up" throughout most of the Adirondacks. ("Yarding up" is the habit of other deer species of congregating in large numbers in relatively small, sheltered locations during the winter months.)

Food: In winter, moose will browse on limbs and bark of mountain ash, cherry, poplar, northern wild raisin and even balsam fir. Researchers have found that plants such as water lilies contain the high sodium content needed to digest other roughage.

Reproduction: The mating season usually occurs in September and October. After a gestation period of about 8 months, 1 or 2 young, called calves for their cow-like appearance, are born in May or June. In the fall, because of the scarcity of females, bulls range up to 50 miles a day in search of a mate.

Comments: The moose is both the largest land animal in the northeast and the largest deer in the world. In Europe, the moose-like deer are known as elk, a name which was misapplied to the native wapiti by early explorers.

After a century of virtual extirpation in which only occasional stragglers entered New York State from Canada or Vermont, moose permanently returned to northern New York in 1980. In 1990, there are an estimated 15-20 animals roaming an area larger than the state of Connecticut, so chances of seeing one are not good. Interestingly, most of the moose entering New York are bulls, so it cannot yet be claimed that a permanent breeding base has been reestablished. Presently, a SUNY College of Environmental Science and Forestry feasibility study is being conducted to analyze the effects of bringing in more moose. Plans are being considered for the release of 40 additional animals, from which it is hoped that our moose population could climb to well over 1,000 animals by early in the next century. Such transplants could roam the mountains by 1991, which could increase all our chances of seeing one of these symbols of the great northwoods wilderness, in addition to hopefully cutting down on the excessive commuting time the lonely bulls are currently enduring.

WHITETAIL DEER
Odocoileus virginianus

Medium-light Brown
Plate 21, No. 1
Plate 22, No. 1, 2, 3 & 4
Plate 23, No. 1, 2, 3 & 4

Total length: 60-72 inches
Height at shoulder: 36-40 inches
Tail: 8-12 inches
Weight: 100-250 pounds

Description: In summer the back, sides, chest and outsides of the legs are bright chestnut to reddish brown. The crown of the head and upper surface of the tail are darker brown, sometimes intermixed with almost black hairs. The nose and eyes are black, and there is a small, almost black patch on each side of the mouth. The nose and eyes are usually ringed with white, and the throat, inside of the ears, inside of the legs, belly and underside of the tail are white. In winter the upper parts of the body become a lighter, duller brown, often grayish brown. The young are bright chestnut red, and covered with white spots the first few months of life.

Habitat: Deer prefer old pasture land and young forests instead of deep wilderness areas where crown cover closes in and shades out ground vegetation. As a result, with increased "forever wild" land, it is unlikely that deer will return to the record high numbers of the 1950's in the central Adirondacks. In winter whitetail deer "yard up." Yarding consists of a large number of deer coming together to pass the winter months in a relatively small but sheltered area, such as dense stands of conifer trees.

Food: In spring, summer and fall when food is plentiful, deer browse on a variety of foods such as grasses and other greens, acorns and other small nuts, and fungi—including the highly regarded morel. Near more settled areas, deer frequent corn fields and apple orchards in search of two of their favorite foods. Twigs and buds of plants such as white cedar are important foods in winter, but if all preferred foods are overbrowsed, deer will even eat balsam fir, a poor food source, in an attempt to survive.

Reproduction: The rut, the deer's mating season, peaks in November. After a gestation period of almost seven months, a pair of fawns, or occasionally triplets, is born in late May.

Comments: The whitetail is named for its large tail, undoubtedly the most frequently observed portion of its anatomy! Bucks may be located in early autumn by "rubs," which are saplings and small trees girdled of bark by bucks rubbing the early velvet sheathing off their horns. Despite occasional claims to the contrary, sighting of large-eared deer in the Adirondacks are not mule deer. Mule deer are a western species that have never existed within hundreds of miles of this area.

Hearing and smell are a deer's most important senses. When frightened, deer can travel as fast as 35 miles an hour. Deer are essentially a southern species, and the Adirondacks are near the northern limit where they can prosper; therefore, winter weather has a tremendous impact on their numbers.

Populations are also affected more than most animal species by hunting pressures. Due to the unexpected efficiency of buck hunters and the legal protection afforded to does (female deer), the New York State deer herd has a disproportionately large doe to buck ratio. In addition, the vast majority of bucks are taken by hunters at an average age of less than two years, only about one quarter of their natural life span. This has led to an unnaturally large population of undersized animals. (This situation is not so extreme within the Adirondack Park where rougher terrain and lower human/hunter population densities allow the average buck to live longer than in less remote areas of the state.) Advanced deer management studies support the theory that the healthiest possible deer herds are achieved by programs that insure both a natural buck to doe ratio and a natural spread of age groups among both sexes.

BLACK BEAR
Ursidae family

BLACK BEAR   Black
Ursus americanus   Plate 24, No. 1 & 2

Total length: 4½ - 5½ feet
Height at shoulder: 2½ -3 feet
Tail: 4-5 inches
Weight: 175-300 pounds

Description: Bears are large, thickset animals, with very short tails. They have elongated muzzles and short rounded ears. Each foot has five fully developed toes, with long non-retractile claws.

The typical coloration of a black bear is black over the entire body except for the muzzle, which is frequently dull brown. There may be a scattering of white hairs on the breast, and in some specimens there are enough of these to form a small blaze. Less frequently, brown bears may be observed, their color ranging from light straw to dark chocolate.

Habitat: Bears are found in wooded areas throughout the Adirondack Park. They frequently live close to human population centers, especially if they can gain access to local garbage supplies. As winter approaches, bears seek out dens, usually in large brush piles or root holes left by falling trees, but they are not true hibernators. Even though their heart rate drops to only one or two beats per minute, their body temperature remains close to normal.

Food: Bears are omnivorous opportunistic feeders whose foods range from small mammals, birds and their eggs, fish and insects to fruit and berries. They also invade bee trees for honey. In some areas of the park, bears have damaged electrical poles after apparently mistaking the buzzing of these lines for that of bees. Most Adirondack dumps have a resident bear population that appears each evening in search of a free meal.

Reproduction: The mating season takes place from June into July. Although mating occurs in midsummer, most growth and development within the womb does not occur until the female dens up in winter. The young cubs, usually twins, are born the following January while the female is still in a state of semi-hibernation. Bear cubs weigh only about ½ pound at birth.

Comments: There are over 3,500 bears in the Adirondacks and chances are good for bear/human encounters. Because of its size, color and shape, few people have trouble identifying it. The black bear is a plantigrade (animal that walks on its entire foot), and its tracks are easily identified. The front or smaller pad is the one most often seen. It can be simulated by making a fist, then pressing down on loose soil or sand. Another bear sign is claw marks (long scratches) on beech trees where a bear has gripped the trunk while climbing in search of nuts. Bear droppings usually contain the clearly visible undigested seeds and pits of cherries, hobbleberries and other fruit.

Should you be fortunate enough to observe a wild bear, remember the old adages concerning such situations: avoid getting between a mother and her cubs and don't feed the bears! People who feed bears are the true culprits responsible when a bear has to be destroyed because it has lost its fear of humans. Although they appear cuddly and harmless, treat them with due respect for their size and power.

MAN
Hominidae family

MAN
Homo sapiens
Height: 5-6 feet
Weight: 100-200 pounds

Light Pinkish Tan to Dark Brown
Plate 25, No. 1

Description: Walks upright on hind limbs. Five fully developed digits on each hand or foot. Body covered with fine hairs, skin color variable from pinkish tan to dark brown. Hair thickest on head, ranging in color from blonde to brown to black, occasionally reddish.

Habitat: Humans may be encountered in any part of the park, but the majority of their dens are restricted to the lower elevations. Dens are usually constructed from forest materials, although occasionally stone or brick is also employed.

Food: Omnivorous, everything from peanut brittle to oat bran.

Reproduction: Humans have a year round breeding season, peaking during blackouts. Following a gestation period of about 9 months, usually a single rather vocal child is produced.

Comments: Increasing in both population and presence within the park boundaries. Originally very aggressive and intolerant of sharing its range with other large animals, although some theories suggest man is now evolving a more social acceptance of other species. Long term studies will be necessary to determine the validity of this observation.

Section IV

Extirpated Species

American Elk
Cervus elaphus

WOLVERINE
Mustelidae family

WOLVERINE   Dark Brown
Gulo luscus   Plate 26, No. 1 & 2

Total length: 30-40 inches
Head and body: 24-31 inches
Tail: 6-9 inches
Weight: 20-30 pounds

Description: Wolverines have stout, bear-like bodies covered with long shaggy hair. They have large heads with short ears. Their legs are short and their tails are short and bushy.

Body, tail and legs are dark brown to blackish brown; undersurface brown. The top and the sides of the head are intermixed with gray hairs. There is a dirty white patch on the throat, and sometimes another on the chest. The feet are black. There is a broad stripe of chestnut to yellowish white hair along each side, the two bands joining above the base of the tail to form a V-shape.

Habitat: The wolverine was previously encountered in both the forests and the more open areas of New York State.

Food: Everything from roots and fruit to birds and their eggs, rodents, porcupines, even snowbound deer. Wolverines have a reputation for being ruthless hunters and ravenous feeders, even entering human habitations in search of food.

Reproduction: In New York State, mating occured during any of the warmer months, although implantation did not take place until late winter. 2 to 4 young were born, usually in April.

Comments: By weight, the wolverine was the largest member of the weasel family in eastern North America. It vanished from the Adirondacks around the late 19th century, a victim of its own bold and fearless character. It is believed that today the nearest wild living wolverines are hundreds of miles outside of New York State. It is interesting to contrast the status of the wolverine with that of its large gray relative, the badger. Because the badgers feeding and living habits lessen the frequency of its contact with man, badgers have lost far less of their original range than the overly bold wolverine. Badgers are not known to have naturally inhabited the Adirondacks, nor are they considered residents of New York State. In spite of this a review of *The Conservationist* magazine documents isolated examples of badgers being found across New York in very recent times. It is believed these wayward animals were previous residents of a failed fur farming business, and not part of an established population.

The wolverine is also known as *Gulo gulo*.

GRAY TIMBER WOLF
Canidae family

GRAY TIMBER WOLF   Medium Gray
Canis lupus   Plate 26, No. 3 & 4

Total length: 54-60 inches
Head and body: 42-45 inches
Tail: 12-15 inches
Height at shoulder: 25-27 inches
Weight: 70-100 pounds

Description: Wolves are large, dog-like in appearance, and have long legs and bushy tails. The heads have elongated, pointed muzzles and upright triangular ears. The feet have dull, non-retractile claws. The hair is long and thick.

The back is covered with long gray, black-tipped hairs, often forming a dark ridge along the backbone. Hairs longest on the back above the forequarters, which the wolf erects when it feels threatened. Sides paler, undersurface whitish. There is a slight intermixing of brownish hairs throughout, most pronounced on the outer surfaces of the legs. Face grayish to whitish overall, often with a brown blaze on the crest of the muzzle. Tail like the back, with a dark ridge on the upper surface and paler, sometimes brownish beneath, and black-tipped. Individual specimens vary widely in color, from paler to reddish brown to almost black.

Habitat: The wolf was primarily an animal of the forest.

Food: Wolves fed primarily on deer, smaller mammals and birds.

Reproduction: The mating season occured from February to March. Following a gestation period of about 63 days, a litter of approximately 6-7 pups was born in April or May.

Comments: Each year there are a number of reported sightings in the Adirondacks. Even dead wolves have been found, though experts believe that they were released pets. Were the real wolf still widespread enough to be well known, presumably the number of false sightings (usually based on large coyotes) would drop dramatically. Occasional stragglers notwithstanding, the Adirondacks have not been home to a breeding population of wolves in some time. Timber wolves did, however, inhabit northern New York until 1899 when the last dead wolf was turned in for bounty money in St. Lawrence County.

Even though there are no current plans for reintroduction, free roaming wolves can be found a mere 60 miles north of the New York-Canadian border. Since packs travel up to 20 miles each evening in search of food, it would appear easy for them, after a few days journey, to repopulate the Adirondacks. There are two major barriers however, the St. Lawrence River and the unfavorable habitat in southern Ontario and Quebec. Interestingly, wolves living in southern Ontario are smaller (65 pounds average weight) than their cousins further north (80-100 pounds). These southern wolves are only 20% larger than some large eastern coyotes.

Timber wolves are social animals, and they travel about in family groupings of five or six, sometimes up to eight. This group includes the mated pair and some offspring, the older male being the dominant leader. Probably their most famous trademark is their howling which is used to establish territory, locate a member, or maintain group unity. Although it is tantalizing to imagine hearing the lonely howl of the timber wolf, the essence of the wilderness, in the Adirondacks, for the present time, it can only remain an echo of the past.

Formerly known as *Canis occidentalis* and *Canis nubilis*.

MOUNTAIN LION
Felidae family

MOUNTAIN LION   Yellowish Brown
Felis concolor   Plate 27, No. 1

Total length: 6-7 feet
Head and body: 4-4³/₄ feet
Tail: 2¹/₂ - 2²/₃ feet
Height at shoulder: 2¹/₂ feet
Weight: 125-175 pounds

Description: The mountain lion has a large cat-like head and body covered with short hair. The tail is long, about ¹/₃ of the total length. The upper parts and sides are usually yellowish brown, sometimes fulvous (yellowish chestnut), or grayish. Color is often darker on the crown, peak of the back and the upper surface of the tail. The undersurface of the tail is grayish brown, tip blackish. The inner surface of the ears is light colored, back surface blackish. There is often a patch of darker coloration at the base of the whiskers. The lips, chin, throat, breast, undersurface and insides of the forelegs are a dirty white. The young are yellowish brown and usually spotted for the first six months of life.

Habitat: Previously they were found throughout the Park, from the valleys to the high peaks.

Food: Mountain lions were known to prey on rodents, deer and even porcupines. After it kills a deer, it will drag the carcass to a safe spot and partially conceal it with leaves and sticks.

Reproduction: The mountain lion's mating season was highly variable, but it probably peaked in late winter. Following a gestation period of 91-97 days, a litter of usually 2 kittens was born anytime from May to July.

Comments: The present status of the mountain lion is frequently the subject of debate in New York State. The one fact that clearly emerges is that whatever its true status, people deeply want to believe that a remnant population still inhabits the more remote areas of the Adirondacks. Fueling this debate are reports by responsible people who believe they have seen one of these cats within the Park. Because it is such a large cat, it seems that the mountain lion (also called cougar, puma, catamount and panther) would easily be identified, yet in the past DEC officials have investigated reported sightings that turned out to be domestic housecats, fishers and even large dogs. Individual specimens have undoubtedly been encountered (Bill having observed one on several occasions around 1970) but it is most probable these cats travelled in from outside New York or were intentional releases. Is there a vestige breeding population of mountain lions left in the Adirondack Park? Until it is documented otherwise, that possibility seems highly unlikely. What is beyond doubt is that the mountain lion remains deeply ingrained in Adirondack lore.

AMERICAN ELK
Cervidae family

AMERICAN ELK   Light Brown
Cervus elaphus   Plate 27, No. 2

Head and Body: 80-100 inches
Height at shoulder: 50-60 inches
Tail: 5-7 inches
Weight: 600-700 pounds

Description: The elk is a large, long-legged deer with generally short body hair and a comically stubby tail. The antlers, which commonly have 12-14 points, reach 45-55 inches in length.

In summer the body is grayish brown to yellowish brown, darkest along the peak of the back. The head and neck are darker brown, and the legs and belly are so dark as to appear almost black. The hairs ringing the eyes, the inside of the ears and the chin are pale brown. The tail and a large patch surrounding it are yellowish, and the lower portion of this patch is bordered by almost black hairs. In winter the body becomes much grayer. Male and female are colored alike, except that in winter the female is even paler than the male. The young are yellowish brown, and covered with dull cream colored spots the first months of life.

Habitat: Elk were residents of the forest and nearby lands.

Food: The elk was a browser, feeding on grass and other green vegetation in summer and twigs and bark in winter.

Reproduction: The elk's mating season peaked in early autumn. After a gestation period of between 8½ and 9 months 1 or 2 young, known alternately as either calves or fawns, were born in late spring.

Comments: The American elk was probably never very numerous in the central Adirondacks. They were more often found in the foothills and valleys until loss of habitat forced them to retreat to higher elevations. Attempts to reintroduce the elk to the Adirondacks earlier in this century were not successful.

The elk is the largest round-antlered deer in the world. It is also sometimes known by the Indian name of wapiti. Formerly listed as *Cervus canadensis*.

HARBOR SEAL
Phocidae family

HARBOR SEAL   Yellowish Gray
Phoca vitulina   Plate 27, No. 3

Total length: 4-5 feet
Tail: 3½-4 inches
Weight: 200-300 pounds

Description: The harbor seal's body is cylindrical, tapering at both ends and covered with hair. Its limbs are modified into fin-like flippers for swimming, the rear flippers closely placed together. All flippers bear claws or nails. Its head is dog-like, with a narrow muzzle, gradually sloping forehead and no visible external ears. The tail is rudimentary.

The body is usually yellowish gray above and a paler yellowish white beneath. Both upper and lower surfaces have some black spotting. A less common color phase is dark brown with lighter colored spots.

Habitat: The seal was a semi-aquatic mammal, and within the Adirondack Park was only found along Lake Champlain.

Food: Fish and shellfish.

Reproduction: The mating season occured in July. Following a gestation period of about 9 months, usually a single pup was born on land in early spring.

Comments: In his *Mammals of the Adirondack Region*, published in 1884, Clinton Hart Marriam describes a population of harbor seals living in Lake Champlain along the eastern border of the park. These seals undoubtedly reached this area by traveling down the St. Lawrence River system. It is a sad commentary of those times that in every seal encounter Marriam describes, the animal was slain solely for the sake of examination.

Also known as the common seal.

WILD BOAR
Suidae family

WILD BOAR
Sus scrofa

Head and body: 4-6 feet
Height at shoulder: 2½-3 feet
Tail: 10-12 inches
Weight: 100-300 pounds

Description: The head and body are pig-like in form and outline, covered with stiff, coarse hairs. The tail hangs down, not coiled as in domesticated stock. "Tusk" teeth of lower jaw unusually long and curved, sometimes visibly protruding from the mouth. Directly above these in the upper jaw are a pair of oversized upturned teeth, more massive than those of the lower jaw but not as long. The boar snaps his jaws together with a loud noise, to sharpen the lower tusks against the larger teeth above.

Feral boar (domesticated stock which have back-bred to their ancestral form) can be any color from pale yellow-brown to jet black or sometimes irregular mixes of these colors. Purebred wild boar which have never been domesticated are more muscular in form and brownish black to black. The coats of older specimens are heavily grizzled, especially around the head and forequarters, with gray hairs. The young are much lighter in color, and covered with irregular markings not unlike those on the surface of a watermelon.

Habitat: Within the Adirondacks, wild boar were found inhabiting semi-open woodlands.

Food: Roots, vegetation, fallen fruit, small animals. Boar fed by uprooting the ground, one reason for their lack of popularity.

Reproduction: There is no record of released wild boar reproducing in New York State. It would be a fair assumption that their reproductive habits would be similar to those in established herds in nearby New Hampshire, where the mating season peaks in mid-winter. Following a gestation period of about 16 weeks, a litter of 8-12 young is born in mid-spring.

Comments: Although not usually associated with the Adirondacks, in his *Adirondack Album*, Volume 1, Barney Fowler reported that in the early 1900's someone attempted to stock wild boar in the Indian Lake region. It was believed that this entire stocking had been killed off by local hunters, although he also reports that in far more recent times, a small population of boar was "rediscovered." Mr. Fowler did not venture an opinion as to whether these boar were feral or original wild stock, but the single photograph I have seen appears to be that of a wild eurasian specimen. The report of a population persisting for some years supports this theory, for it is highly unlikely the feral type could survive the severe Adirondack winter. Purebred wild boar have existed in and near Corbin Park in the mountains of New Hampshire for decades, a testament to their hardy character.

Section V

Footprints and Tracks

Lynx
Lynx canadensis

SHREWS

All four prints: ¼″ L x ¼″ W

VOLES

All four prints: ½″ L x ½″ W

BOG LEMMING

All four prints: ½″ L x ½″ W

WHITE-FOOTED MICE

All four prints: ³⁄₈″ L x ³⁄₈″ W

JUMPING MICE

Front print: ³⁄₈″ L x ³⁄₈″ W
Hind print: 1³⁄₈″ L x ¹⁄₂″ W

OLD WORLD RAT

All four prints: 1″ L x 1″ W

BEAVER

Front print: 2½-3½″ L x 2-2½″ W
Hind print: 5-6½″ L x 4-5″ W; shows webbing

OPOSSUM

Front print: slightly less than 2″ L x 2″ W
Hind print: 2″ L x 2″ W

MUSKRAT

Front print: 1¼-1½″ L x 1¼-1½″ W
Hind print: 2-3″ L x 1½-1¾″ W

SNOWSHOE HARE

Front print: 5-6″ L x 3½-4″ W
Hind print: 1¾″ L x 1½″ W

COTTONTAILS

Front print: 1″ L x 1″ W
Hind print: 3-3½″ L x 1″ W

Comments: Tracks of the Rabbit family show four toes on the rear feet and five toes on the front feet. Rabbit tracks typically exhibit the triangular pattern shown above with the front feet appearing last due to the way rabbits move.

SQUIRRELS

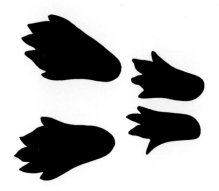

WOODCHUCK

Front print: 1¼-1½″ L x 1¼-1½″ W
Hind print: 1¾-2″ L x 1¼″ W

RED SQUIRREL

Front print: ½″ L x ½″ W
Hind print: 1-1½″ L x ½″ W

GRAY SQUIRREL

Front print: 1″ L x 1″ W
Hind print: 2-2½″ L x 1″ W

CHIPMUNK

Front print: ¼″ L x ¼″ W
Hind print: 1-1½″ L x ½″ W

Tracks of the Squirrel family show five toes on the larger
hind feet and four toes on the smaller front feet. Tracks typically
exhibit the box-like pattern shown above.

FLYING SQUIRREL

Front print: ½″ L x ½″ W
Hind print: 1-1½″ L x ½″ W

May be differentiated from Red Squirrel prints by imprint of the
gliding membrane connecting the front and hind feet.

CANINES

COYOTE

All four prints: 2¼-2½″ L x 2-2¼″ W

RED FOX

All four prints: 2″ L x 1¾-2″ W

GRAY FOX

All four prints: 1½-1¾″ L x 1¼-1½″ W

Tracks of the Canine family show four toes with claw marks evident.

FELINES

BOBCAT

All four prints: 1¾-2″ L x 1½-1¾″ W

LYNX

All four prints: 3″ L x 3½″ W; appear larger in winter

The bobcat and lynx show four toes; claw marks usually not visible.

PORCUPINE

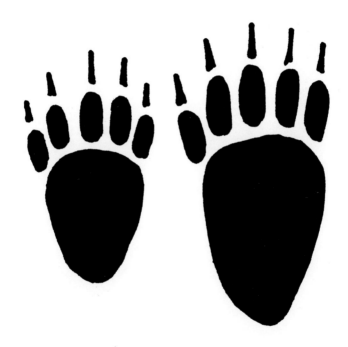

Front print: 2½-2¾″ L x 1¼-1½″ W
Hind print: 3-4″ L x 1½-2″ W

RACCOON

Front print: 2½″ L x 2¼″ W
Hind print: 4″ L x 2¼″ W

WEASELS

STRIPED SKUNK

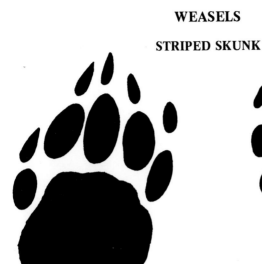

Front print: 2″ L x 1½″ W
Hind print: 2-2½″ L x 1¼″ W

MINK

All four prints: 1½-1¾″ L x 1½-1¾″ W

OTTER

Front print: 2½″ L x 2½″ W
Hind print: 2¼-3¾″ L x 2½-4″ W; shows webbing between toes

WEASELS

FISHER

All four prints: 2½-3½" L x 2¼-3¼" W

MARTEN

All four prints: 1½-1¾" L x 1¼-1½" W

LONG-TAILED WEASEL

Front print: ½-¾" L x ½-¾" W
Hind print: 1-1½" L x ½-¾" W

SHORT-TAILED WEASEL

Front print: ½-¾" L x ½-¾" W
Hind print: 1" L x ¾" W

Tracks of the above members of the Weasel family may exhibit the box-like pattern of the squirrels or the triangular pattern of the rabbits. The weasels differ by showing five toes on both front and hind feet.

DEER

MOOSE

All four prints: 6-7″ L x 5-6″ W

Track up to 10″ long if dewclaw imprints are showing.

WHITETAIL DEER

All four prints: 2¾-3½″ L x 2-2¾″ W

Track up to 5½″ long if dewclaw imprints are showing.

BLACK BEAR

Front print: 3½-4″ L x 3¼-3¾″ W
Hind print: 6½-7″ L x 6¼-6¾″ W

MAN

Typical print: 8-13″ L x 2-4″ W

MAKING CASTS OF ANIMALS TRACKS

Making plaster casts of animal tracks is a good way to identify the wildlife in your area and is a fun activity for almost any age level. The only materials needed are plaster of Paris, strips of cardboard (some 2″ and some 4″ wide and about 12″ to 24″ long, depending on the size of the track), an empty half gallon milk container, a mixing spoon, a can of vegetable cooking spray, water and, of course, a clear animal track. The best prints can be found in soft mud near a stream or on a woodland trail after a rain. Simply mix the plaster of Paris with water to a creamy consistency, make a ring out of the 2″ cardboard to fit around the track and very carefully pour in the plaster. Let it dry about two hours or so, depending on how wet the dirt is.

When the plaster is completely dry, lift it up, take the cardboard wrapping off and carefully wipe off the mud. You now have an exact pattern with which to make a cast of the animal's track. Now, spray the pattern with vegetable spray (rubbing it with softened soap will do also) and lay it face up on a flat surface. Then wrap another wider strip of cardboard around it and fasten securely. Pour in fresh plaster and let dry thoroughly (about 2 to 3 hours). When you unwrap the cardboard and separate the casts you will have an exact replica of the original animal track. These casts can be painted and labeled to make an interesting collection.

—Kathleen Aprill

INJURED AND ORPHANED WILDLIFE*

One of the most common questions I hear is what to do if one should come across injured or orphaned wildlife. In the case of "orphaned" wildlife, it is usually best to do nothing! Unless you actually find the body of the parent animal, do not assume that any young animals you find are either orphaned or in need of human assistance—no matter how small or helpless they appear to you. Very young animals are frequently left alone for a time while the parent is out seeking food. The natural parent best prepares an animal for life in the wild, so unless you know the parent has died, the greatest kindness you can do young wildlife you encounter is to leave them alone.

One possible exception that occasionally occurs is finding a baby squirrel that is clearly too young to care for itself that has fallen from its nest. You can put it in a cardboard box with a warm cloth and place the box at the foot of the tree so that the mother can retrieve her baby. If the mother has not come for the baby in about two hours, you may want to call a wildlife rehabilitator for further suggestions. In this case, it is not a good idea to leave the baby outside all night.

Another special case you will want to be aware of concerns the opossum. Female opossums have a pouch that they carry their babies in. If you see a dead opossum by the side of the road in the spring, she may be dead but the babies may be alive. Please check. The pouch is on the stomach toward the back legs. Should you find living young, contact the DEC for a wildlife rehabilitator at once.

Remember, in New York State it is illegal for an unlicensed citizen to possess wildlife. The DEC (Department of Environmental Conservation) licenses specially trained wildlife rehabilitators who volunteer enormous amounts of time and expertise to care for orphaned and injured wildlife. Wherever possible, they do this in a way that permits the animal to be returned to the wild. Where this is not possible, they find a permanent home for disabled animals. Should you find an animal in need of assistance, contact your regional office of the DEC to be put in touch with the nearest qualified wildlife rehabilitator.

* Our thanks to Judy Cusworth of the Woodhaven Wildlife Center for special assistance in preparing this information.

RABIES*

Anyone interested in and spending time near wildlife should have some knowledge of the threat of rabies. Rabies is a viral infection carried by various mammals, and unless promptly treated it is a fatal infection. An animal infected with rabies may exhibit atypical behavior ranging from disorientation to aggression. Although transmission of the rabies virus is best known to occur from being bitten by a rabid animal, rabies can also be contracted through cuts or scratches from handling a rabid animal, even if it is already dead. Should you be bitten or come in contact with a potential rabies carrier, wash the area well with soap and see a doctor immediately. If possible, keep the suspect animal confined. A trained technician can identify rabies in an animal by examining the brain tissue.

In recent years bats have been the biggest carrier of rabies in New York State. Interestingly, most of the infected bats were big brown bats, *Eptesicus fuscus*. In the country as a whole, skunks and raccoons account for the majority of confirmed rabies cases, followed by bats in third place. Fox, livestock, dogs and cats also have been found to carry rabies. It seems that rabies increases and decreases in distinct cycles within each of these groups. Using the raccoon as an example, although no rabid raccoons were recorded in New York State in 1989, it is expected that a wave of infection moving up from the south will account for about 30 cases of raccoon rabies in 1990, with even more predicted for the years immediately following.

Because the threat of rabies is very real in our area, use all possible care in dealing with wild animals, especially bats, raccoons, skunks, and foxes. If you suspect rabies, immediately contact the Rabies Laboratory of the State of New York Department of Health.

* We wish to thank the staff of the DOH Rabies Laboratory in Albany for providing assistance and information concerning the status of rabies in New York State.

AFTERWORD

One fact that clearly emerges from examining the life histories of the wild mammals is that, for better or for worse, man has become a major influence on their world.

At the present time it is refreshing to find groups involved and working together to correct past mistakes and protect the Adirondack Park's future. The attempt to reintroduce the lynx has required the skills and services of educators and students, state and local officials, Yukon trappers and New York naturalists, each contributing their share to make that project possible.

In another part of the Adirondack wilderness there lives a colony of beavers who once made their home alongside a shopping center, threatening its drainage system with their dams. It took an unlikely alliance among wildlife rehabilitators, a local trappers association, preservationists and politicians to capture and relocate the entire colony to a new environment better suited to the beaver's needs.

Examples such as these illustrate man's interest in and concern for wild animals. Another indication of the depth of these feelings is the amount of research and studies carried out to help us better understand the natural world. Both professional and nonprofessional residents of the Adirondack Park are in the position of being asked to contribute opinions and potential support on issues such as species reintroduction and habitat preservation.

For all persons interested in wildlife management for quality of life (as opposed to quantity), we strongly recommend reading all available information on this subject. As the premier influence on the natural world, it is essential we learn as much as possible about the consequences of our actions upon wild populations of all other species of animals.

INDEX TO COMMON NAMES

INDEX TO LATIN NAMES

158

GLOSSARY

Arboreal - Living in or frequently inhabiting trees. Examples: Fishers, squirrels.

Boreal - Related to the northern areas of the continent.

Deer Yard - A somewhat sheltered area where large numbers of deer congregate during harsh winter weather.

Extirpate - To completely remove or destroy an animal population from a given area. Example: Elk in the Adirondacks.

Fulvous - Yellowish red.

Grizzled - An intermixing of gray with a base color. Example: Fur of the opossum.

Mammary Glands - The breasts of a mammal which provide milk for the young.

Melanistic - Word describing an animal exhibiting an overabundance of the dark pigment melanin, causing the animal to appear black.

Plantigrade - An animal which walks with the entire sole of the foot in contact with the ground. Examples: Man, raccoon, bear, skunk.

Prehensile - Adapted for grasping or seizing.

Rufous - Reddish.

Sign - Physical evidence of an animal's presence. Example: Footprints.

Understory - The lower levels of vegetative growth in a forest; below the trees.